AI for Utilities

Reimagining the Future Energy System

Dr. Debashish Roy

Apress®

AI for Utilities: Reimagining the Future Energy System

Dr. Debashish Roy
San Diego, CA, USA

ISBN-13 (pbk): 979-8-8688-0201-0   ISBN-13 (electronic): 979-8-8688-0202-7
https://doi.org/10.1007/979-8-8688-0202-7

Managing Director, Apress Media LLC: Welmoed Spahr
Acquisitions Editor: Susan McDermott
Development Editor: Laura Berendson
Project Manager: Jessica Vakili

Cover designed by eStudioCalamar

Distributed to the book trade worldwide by Apress Media, LLC, 1 New York Plaza, New York, NY 10004, U.S.A. Phone 1-800-SPRINGER, fax (201) 348-4505, e-mail orders-ny@springer-sbm.com, or visit www.springeronline.com. Apress Media, LLC is a California LLC and the sole member (owner) is Springer Science + Business Media Finance Inc (SSBM Finance Inc). SSBM Finance Inc is a **Delaware** corporation.

For information on translations, please e-mail booktranslations@springernature.com; for reprint, paperback, or audio rights, please e-mail bookpermissions@springernature.com.

Apress titles may be purchased in bulk for academic, corporate, or promotional use. eBook versions and licenses are also available for most titles. For more information, reference our Print and eBook Bulk Sales web page at http://www.apress.com/bulk-sales.

Any source code or other supplementary material referenced by the author in this book is available to readers on GitHub (https://github.com/Apress). For more detailed information, please visit https://www.apress.com/gp/services/source-code.

If disposing of this product, please recycle the paper

Table of Contents

About the Author

Dr. Debashish Roy has emerged as a luminary in the realm of Technology Innovation Leadership, particularly within the utility industry, boasting nearly 16 years of distinguished service. His tenure is marked by a profound commitment to harnessing the potential of digital, cloud, AI/ML, and analytics to catalyze significant business transformations for Fortune 500 organizations. As a Technology Leader within the Technology Advisory and Client Delivery sector of a premier Fortune 500 company since 2010, Dr. Roy has made indelible strides in the utility sector, demonstrating an unmatched prowess in addressing complex industry challenges and championing innovation.

His tenure includes the development and implementation of pioneering solutions in AI, machine learning, and cloud technologies, which have been instrumental in propelling business visions and enhancing operational efficiencies. Dr. Roy's dedication to AI for sustainable development is particularly noteworthy, emphasized by his doctoral research and the development of over ten AI-powered patents. This commitment positions him as a respected thought leader in the field.

This book encapsulates Dr. Roy's journey of transformative leadership and his unwavering commitment to advancing sustainable, AI-driven solutions within the utility sector, setting a benchmark for innovation and excellence.

Acknowledgments

I am deeply grateful to all those who have supported me on the journey of writing this book. First, I would like to express my heartfelt thanks to my family, whose unwavering support and encouragement have been my anchor and inspiration throughout this process.

A special word of appreciation goes to my colleagues and mentors in the industry, whose insights and expertise have greatly enriched the content of this book. Their willingness to share their knowledge and experience has been invaluable.

I also extend my gratitude to my friends, for their patience, understanding, and for the countless ways they have offered their support during the writing of this book.

Lastly, but importantly, I thank you, the reader, for your interest in this work. It is my sincere hope that it will inspire, inform, and engage you in equal measure. Thank you all for being part of this journey.

Preface: Author's Note

When considering the industries that have significantly advanced human development and shaped modern society, the utility industry stands out as a cornerstone. This sector, encompassing electricity, water, gas, and waste management, forms the bedrock upon which countless other industries and daily activities rely. From powering homes and businesses to ensuring clean drinking water and effective waste disposal, utilities are integral to our quality of life and economic progress. Without the reliable infrastructure provided by this industry, many of the advancements and conveniences we take for granted today would be impossible. This is one of the oldest industries still rapidly growing in the contemporary world.

While the benefits we reap from this industry are abundant, it also poses arduous challenges. While the benefits of the utility industry are immense and far-reaching, including reliable access to electricity, water, and gas, it also faces significant challenges that impact both its effectiveness and sustainability. For instance, the industry must navigate the complexities of maintaining aging infrastructure, managing environmental impacts, and meeting the growing demand for resources in an increasingly urbanized world. Additionally, ensuring equitable access and affordability while investing in innovative technologies presents ongoing hurdles. Addressing these challenges is crucial to maintaining the industry's vital role in supporting modern life and driving future progress. Our planet is unique, and so are the challenges we face. We are currently at a critical juncture where we must decide how to create a sustainable planet for the future. The biggest challenges the utility industry faces is embracing clean energy, building energy-efficient devices, eliminating energy poverty, and paving the way for the next era. Through my 18+ years of deep research and experience working with this industry, I have witnessed the challenges, opportunities, and leverage this industry has. As we move toward an electric decade – a period characterized by the significant shift toward electrification across various sectors, including the widespread adoption of electric vehicles and renewable energy sources – the role of utilities will become much more critical in supporting global climate goals. This period is also marked by the energy transition, which refers to the global shift from fossil-based energy systems to renewable energy sources like wind, solar, and hydro, aimed at reducing carbon emissions and mitigating climate change. Utilities will need to support this transition while managing increased demand, surges in the adoption of smart appliances, and the expansion of decentralized operating systems. Utilities are exploring how to embrace AI to transform their traditional business, create future opportunities and innovate new business models. But the big question for utility executives is to know how they can align utility business transformation and AI in this journey.

The new book, *AI for Utilities*, demystifies how business transformation and AI will join forces in plain-spoken language, revealing a clear roadmap for any utility leader looking to leverage the power of AI to transition their organization into Utility 4.0.

Utilities have undergone significant transformations over the decades, evolving from Utility 1.0, which focused on basic electrification and infrastructure development, to Utility 2.0, characterized by the introduction of automation and early digital technologies to improve operational efficiency. Utility 3.0 brought about more sophisticated digitalization, integrating smart grids, renewable energy sources, and enhanced customer engagement tools.

Now, as we face the unique challenges of the modern era – such as climate change, increased demand for energy, and the decentralization of energy systems – there is a need for a new way of thinking about utilities. Utility 4.0 represents this next phase, where advanced data analytics, AI, and machine learning enable utilities to optimize operations, predict and manage energy demands more effectively, and create more resilient and sustainable energy systems. The integration of AI in this context is opening new opportunities for business transformation, making it a pivotal force in guiding utilities through the complexities of the 21st century.

Forces Shaping the Future of the Utility Industry

The utility industry is uniquely positioned in the fourth industrial revolution era. This industry is well-positioned to transform itself in a way that will enable it to survive and prosper in this era. It has its fair share of challenges, but the opportunities are immense. As new technology and business models emerge, the sector must embrace and leverage them to build a more resilient, efficient, and customer-focused industry.

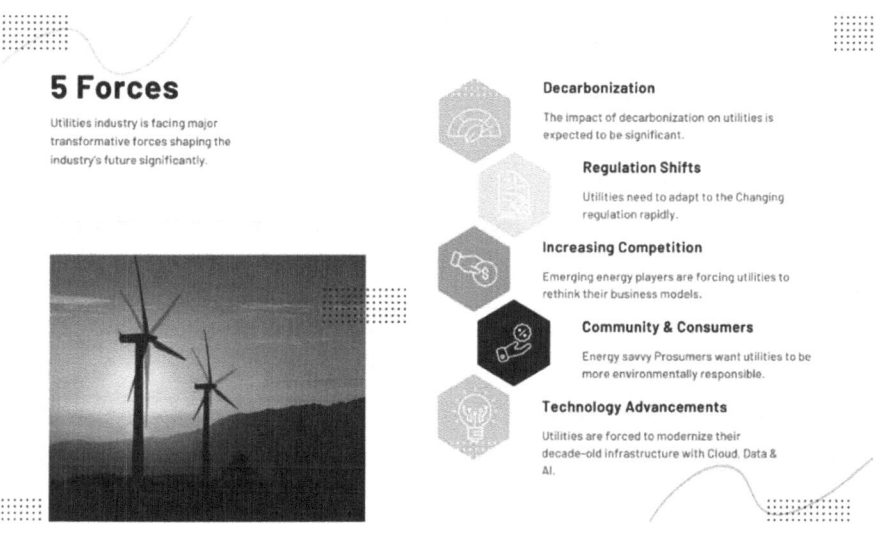

5 Forces

Utilities industry is facing major transformative forces shaping the industry's future significantly.

Decarbonization

The impact of decarbonization on utilities is expected to be significant.

Regulation Shifts

Utilities need to adapt to the Changing regulation rapidly.

Increasing Competition

Emerging energy players are forcing utilities to rethink their business models.

Community & Consumers

Energy savvy Prosumers want utilities to be more environmentally responsible.

Technology Advancements

Utilities are forced to modernize their decade-old infrastructure with Cloud, Data & AI.

5 Advantages Utilities Should Leverage

5 Leverages

Utilities have unique strengths that will help them transform during this new energy era.

Engineering Talent
World-class engineering talent operate the complex energy systems

Customer Base
Utilities have one of the largest customer bases in the services industry.

Network
Utilities companies have the most complex system developed by the human species

Data
Data is the most valuable byproduct generated by the energy ecosystem

Platform
Utilities are very efficient in running the energy platform.

5 Opportunities Ahead of Utilities

5 Opportunities

Energy transition and net zero initiatives providing unique opportunities for the utility industry to emerge as an innovative player.

Energy Diversification
Diversifying the energy sources is a big opportunity for the utilities Industry

New Partnership
Utilities must form new partnerships to emerge as connected energy service providers.

Invest in Future Network
Building the foundation for future networks with the power of 5G

Monetize Data
Developing a monetization strategy is critical for growth.

Expanding into new markets
Utilities should invent new business models and explore untapped potential.

CHAPTER 1

AI for Utilities

Electricity has become an indispensable necessity for modern life. Cutting off access to reliable power, our lives would revert to grueling days, like before the industrial revolution. Perhaps, Hobbes described the state accurately when he said it would be "solitary, poor, nasty, brutish, and short."

Today, almost every feature of modern civilization depends on affordable, reliable electricity and the things it powers, like lamps and heaters. From keeping our homes well-lit and comfortable, powering smartphones to stay in touch with loved ones and sourcing those 24/7 data centers to give us reliable Internet speed, among countless others, the utilities of electrical power run large.

It isn't a false notion to claim that the history of electricity is the history of the modern world.

The utility sector refers to the businesses and industries that provide essential services to the public, such as electricity, gas, water, and telecommunications. These companies typically operate as regulated monopolies, with prices and services set by government agencies. The utility sector aims to provide customers safe, reliable, and affordable services. It is considered a critical infrastructure sector, as its services are essential for daily life and economic activity. The utility sector plays a critical role in our daily lives by providing essential services that support

© Debashish Roy 2024
D. Roy, *AI for Utilities*, https://doi.org/10.1007/979-8-8688-0202-7_1

our basic needs and activities. Some critical ways the utility sector impacts our lives are

1. **Energy**: The utility sector provides electricity that powers our homes, businesses, and public spaces, enabling us to live, work, and play comfortably and conveniently.

2. **Water**: The utility sector manages the treatment and distribution of water, which is essential for drinking, cooking, cleaning, and other daily activities.

3. **Telecommunications**: The utility sector provides the infrastructure for telecommunications services, including telephone, Internet, and television, which are critical for communication, entertainment, and commerce.

4. **Waste management**: The utility sector is responsible for collecting and disposing waste and preserving public health and the environment.

In summary, the utility sector plays a vital role in supporting our daily lives, maintaining public health and safety, and enabling economic growth and prosperity.

History of Electricity

The modern electric utility industry in the United States can be traced to the invention of the practical light bulb in 1879 by Thomas Alva Edison. So, while Edison developed Direct Current (DC), which runs continually in a single direction, like in a battery or a fuel cell, Nikola Tesla introduced the world to Alternative Current (AC). While DC is not easily converted to higher or lower voltages, AC can be converted to different voltages relatively easily using a transformer. Nikola Tesla and Thomas Edison were electrical engineering titans whose inventions changed history. But the world is aware of the electricity that is fueled between the two.

The "war" was marked by a series of events, including Edison's public demonstrations of the dangers of AC and the successful electrification of the 1893 World Columbian Exposition in Chicago using Westinghouse's AC system. Ultimately, AC emerged as the dominant power transmission system and is still used worldwide. Tesla's concept meant that electricity generated in power plants could be converted to high voltage and transmitted over long distances with minimal energy loss. Once it arrives at its destination, distributing it at medium and low voltage using transformers would be simple and inexpensive. This system is currently used to deliver energy from a power station to our home.

Almost every aspect of modern society depends on affordable and dependable electricity, the things it powers, from lamps and heaters to safely keep our homes well-lit and comfortable to smartphones that keep us connected with loved ones and always-on data centers give us reliable Internet – among countless others. It is so crucial to modern life that electricity is the history of the modern world.

Utility Industry

The utility sector is a broad industry that encompasses producing, distributing, and delivering energy and water resources to residential, commercial, and industrial customers. This sector includes a wide range of activities, such as the generation of electricity from fossil fuels, nuclear energy, and renewable sources; the transmission and distribution of electricity through power grids; and the provision of water, gas, and sewage services. The utility sector is essential for the functioning of modern society and plays a critical role in driving economic growth and development.

Business transformation plans that leverage the power of artificial intelligence (AI) can help utility leaders drive operational efficiency, improve customer service, and reduce costs. AI can be applied in various areas within the utility sector, including demand-side management, asset management, grid optimization, and predictive maintenance. As a result, utility organizations may better satisfy the evolving needs of their customers and maintain their competitiveness in an increasingly digital world by implementing AI-driven technologies and procedures.

Environmental Threats Posed by Energy Expansion

Over the past century, global population growth and urbanization have increased energy demand, rapid electrification, and energy consumption. This has negatively impacted our planet and placed us in a dire situation regarding climate change and greenhouse gas emissions. The warming world is getting closer to passing a temperature limit set by global leaders five years ago. According to a new United Nations report, it may exceed it in the next decade (United in Science, 2020). According to the research published by the UN and World Meteorological Organization, greenhouse gas concentrations have continued to grow. They have reached new record highs this year despite already being at their highest levels in three million years. Energy contributes to climate change, accounting for around 60% of global greenhouse gas emissions (Tracking SDG 7 | Progress Towards Sustainable Energy, 2019).

California, which aims to have a carbon-free power grid within 25 years, saw that possibility. The state's primary grid ran on more than 97% renewable energy at 3:39 p.m. on Sunday, April 3, 2022, breaking a previous record of 96.4% set just a week earlier.

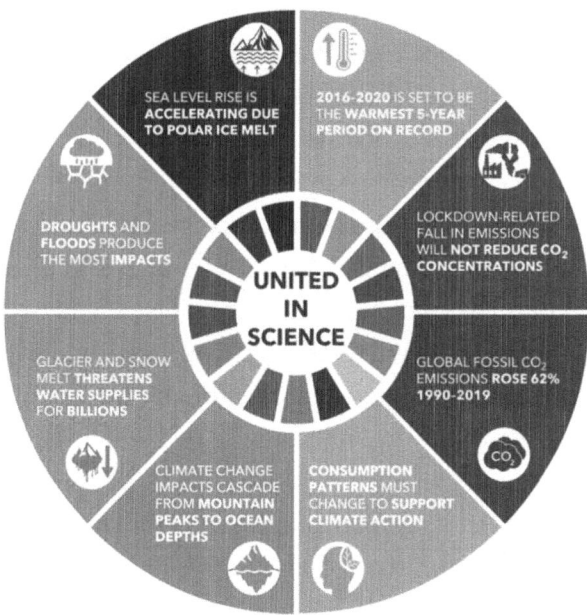

Figure 1-1. *Key messages from United in Science report (2020)*
(United in Science 2020)

On the other hand, the Energy Progress Report (2019) published
by the International energy agency highlighted that a little more than 3
billion people still use wood, coal, charcoal, or animal dung for cooking
and heating, making up 13% of the world's population. Global leaders
and international agencies are simultaneously addressing global warming
and energy poverty issues. They acknowledge that strategies to eradicate
energy poverty must engage with climate risks and opportunities to
achieve sustainable development outcomes. The International Energy
Agency advocates decentralized, medium- and small-scale renewable
energy solutions as the most flexible and cost-effective mechanism for
meeting the energy needs of up to three-quarters of unserved households.
The COP 21 meeting in 2015 resulted in a global agreement to tackle
climate change, known as the Paris Agreement. Two overall development

actions were defined: mitigating greenhouse gas emissions into the atmosphere and adapting to climate change-related disturbances. Adaptation actions include creating resilient infrastructures that will withstand extreme weather and disasters.

Focusing on clean energy research, developing, and promoting renewable energy, energy efficiency, advanced and cleaner fossil fuel technologies, and investment in energy infrastructure, microgrids, and clean energy technology can help tackle problems related to climate change and energy poverty. Furthermore, to optimize energy generation, distribution, and consumption, the utility industry can be transformed by using sophisticated software solutions created with AI and machine learning.

The benefits of achieving the overall energy transformation are countless. Energy and climate goals are closely interlinked and complementary pursuits (Energy Progress Report (2019).

New Market Entrants Are Upending the Utility Business Model

New market entrants are upending the utility business model based on electricity sales and creating new ways for customers to manage their electricity use and costs. In a report titled *Utilities Under Pressure: Disruptive Forces Reshaping the Electric Power Industry*, the analysts identify five forces that are reshaping the utility industry:

- New competitors are challenging the monopoly business model.

- Consumers are taking more control over their electricity.

- Distributed energy resources are growing in scale and scope.

- The electric power sector is undergoing a digital transformation.

- Electric vehicles are poised to transform the auto industry.

The research observes that utilities are investing in new business models and technology in response to these dynamics. Still, it warns that they must do more to adapt to the evolving landscape.

Global Warming and Greenhouse Gas Emissions

Gases that trap heat in the atmosphere are called greenhouse gases. (US EPA, 2017). Greenhouse gases have far-ranging environmental and health effects. They cause climate change by trapping heat and contribute to respiratory disease from smog and air pollution. Extreme weather, food supply disruptions, and increased wildfires are other effects of climate change caused by greenhouse gases. In 2018, US greenhouse gas emissions totaled 6677 million metric tons of carbon dioxide equivalents, or 5903 million metric tons of carbon dioxide equivalents after accounting for sequestration from the land sector. (US EPA, 2017)

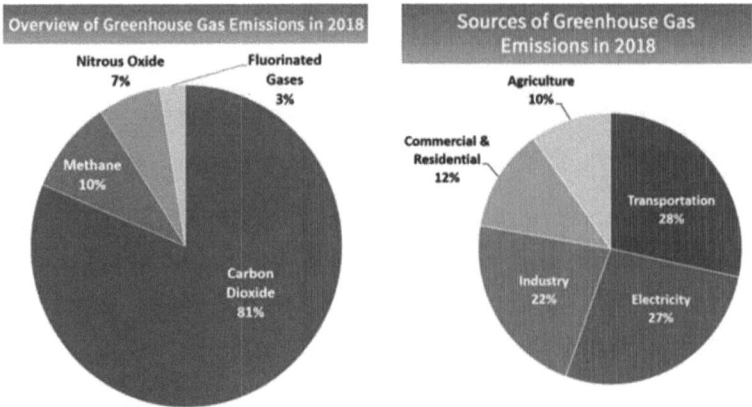

Figure 1-2. *Greenhouse Gas emissions and sources (US EPA, 2017)*

In the United States, 27% of greenhouse gas comes from the electricity sector (US EPA, 2017). The electric grid comprises three major sectors: generation, transmission and distribution, and consumption. Smart generation includes the use of renewable energy sources (wind, solar, or hydropower), which has the potential to decrease overall greenhouse gas emissions by reducing coal and fossil fuel usage for power generation (Abdallah & El-Shennawy, 2013).

Energy Poverty

Rural areas are home to over two-thirds of the world's impoverished population. The eradication of rural poverty depends on increased access to goods, services, and information, as detailed in the United Nations Millennium Development Goals. However, alleviating poverty is hindered by two interlinked phenomena: lack of access to improved energy services and worsening environmental shocks due to climate change. "Energy poverty" also frequently indicates household energy deprivation issues. This concept has traditionally been used to capture the problems of inadequate access to energy in developing countries, involving economic, infrastructural, social equity, education, and health concerns. However, community microgrid initiatives are gaining traction to solve the issues of energy poverty and offer dependable, affordable grid connectivity to regions that are still disconnected due to technical or financial difficulties.

Clean Energy Revolution

As civilization progressed, more and more advanced energy sources were utilized. Coal became the primary energy source in the 19th and 20th centuries, followed by oil and natural gas. These fossil fuels have gradually replaced firewood as the primary source of energy. Since they have a higher energy density, they are also more efficient. However, they also have several disadvantages. Firstly, they are non-renewable resources and will eventually run out. Secondly, they release harmful pollutants into the atmosphere when burned, leading to air pollution. Renewable energy sources, including solar, wind, and hydropower, are gaining importance as the world works to lessen its reliance on fossil fuels. These renewable energy sources do not release harmful pollutants into the atmosphere.

There has been a growing interest in using nuclear power as an energy source in recent years. However, nuclear power plants require a significant investment in upfront capital costs for building and construction, which can take several years to complete. The high capital costs are due to the complex nature of nuclear power generation, which requires specialized equipment and materials and strict safety regulations.

However, once a nuclear power plant is operational, the costs of running and maintaining it are relatively low and stable. Nuclear fuel is relatively inexpensive compared to other energy sources, and the operational costs are relatively consistent over time.

Despite these advantages, the payback period for a nuclear power plant investment is typically lengthy due to the high upfront capital costs and the long construction period. As a result, the payback period can be several decades, making nuclear power a long-term investment.

The upside is that nuclear power plants do not release greenhouse gases into the atmosphere, making them a desirable option for those concerned about climate change. However, nuclear power plants also have some disadvantages. Firstly, they require a large amount of initial investment. Secondly, they produce radioactive waste that must be stored safely for thousands of years. And finally, the type of energy source that is used will have a significant impact on air pollution levels. The most significant effect on the environment stems from the destructive process of uranium mining. Not to forget, nuclear power plants heavily depend on thorium and uranium to generate electricity, and their scarcity is one of the biggest challenges faced by the industry.

On the one hand, fossil fuels, such as coal and oil, release harmful pollutants into the atmosphere when burned. On the other hand, nuclear power plants do not release harmful pollutants into the atmosphere but produce radioactive waste. However, renewable energy sources like solar and wind power, do not release pollutants into the atmosphere.

Over a decade, the capitalized cost of generating solar energy has dropped to one-sixth of what it was in 2005. However, I believe it will not be long until solar energy generation is economically cheaper than thermal power generation worldwide.

AI in the Utility Industry

As the world progresses, many businesses start incorporating artificial intelligence (AI) into their operating strategies to stay competitive. The utility industry is no different. AI is becoming increasingly important for utilities as they look for ways to improve efficiency and better serve their customers. There are several ways that utilities can use AI. For example, AI can help predict maintenance needs and outages. To accomplish this, data gathered by sensors and other devices is analyzed to find trends that might point to a problem. AI can also be used to help manage customer data. This includes things like analyzing customer usage patterns and helping identify potential savings areas. As a result, AI will become even more critical for utilities as they look to improve efficiency and better serve their customers.

As businesses strive to increase efficiency and better serve their consumers, we anticipate that AI will play a more significant role in the utility sector over the coming years. As utilities adopt AI technology, we expect to see improvements in the accuracy of predictions for things like power outages and demand, as well as more personalized customer service and automated processes.

The utility industry is highly regulated, and AI technology is still evolving. Utilities should be cognizant of potential risks, such as cybersecurity threats and issues with regulatory compliance, as they consider implementing AI. Additionally, utilities must consider how AI will affect their workforce. AI has the potential to automate many of the tasks currently performed by humans, which could result in job losses. Therefore, utilities need to be prepared to retrain their workforce for the jobs of the future.

The opportunities for utilities to leverage AI are endless. Utilities can use AI to enhance customer service, streamline grid operations, cut costs, and do much more. In addition, embracing AI will put utilities in a good position to handle future difficulties.

Outline of the Chapters

To be clear, this is not a strategy or AI technical book. In this book, the utility sector is discussed in terms of how it is rapidly changing, what is influencing its future, and how technology, notably AI, is influencing it. If you're in the utility industry, this book is for you. It will provide insights into how the industry is evolving and how AI can improve operations and create new opportunities.

- We talk about the utility industry's future in Chapter 2 to set up the context.

- In Chapter 3, we delve into the multi-dimensional massive transformation in the utility industry, which is building digital DNA.

- This strategic digital DNA segues directly into Chapter 4, where we discuss the AI adoption in the industry, which is at the heart of this transformation.

- In Chapter 5, we explain the Sustainability imperative for the utility industry and how government regulation, consumer and shareholder demand, decreasing the cost of renewables, and social obligations drive this.

- Chapter 6 discusses power generation in the new low-carbon economy.

- Chapter 7 talks about the Microgrid, one of the essential elements of the new low-carbon economy, and its impact.

- In Chapter 8, we will discuss the intelligent transmission and distribution of the future and how AI will shape this journey.

- Evolving utilities retail market, customer demands, and various AI use cases are discussed in Chapter 9.

- Chapter 10 emphasizes the transformational power of electric vehicles and how AI will help with this.

- Chapter 11 focuses on the increasing penetration of distributed energy resources in the grid system, and powerful AI use cases transforming the DER integration.

- Finally, Chapter 12 gives a glimpse of the metaverse technology and its potential impacts on the utility industry.

I hope that with this book, I am putting useful guidance and a future map in your hands on how one of the oldest industries in the world is getting transformed with the power of AI.

CHAPTER 2

Utilities of the Future

This chapter introduces the utility of the future, the Intelligent energy ecosystem, trends expediting the energy transition and moving toward the electric decade, and the role AI will play in this.

Introduction

As the world becomes increasingly interconnected, the demand for controlling and monitoring energy consumption is rising. This growing demand underscores the importance of expanding storage capabilities and enhancing the electric grid infrastructure in the United States. Expanded storage is essential to manage the variability of renewable energy sources, ensuring a stable supply even when demand fluctuates. However, infrastructure improvements alone are not sufficient. Increasing the adoption of smart meters and other digital technologies would provide utilities with real-time data on energy usage, allowing them to better understand and respond to customer demands, optimize energy distribution, and implement more effective demand response strategies.

There are further strategies to lower our energy consumption. For instance, we could alter the layout of our house to promote the usage of energy-efficient heating and cooling equipment. Or consider investing in a programmable thermostat that allows us to adjust our heating and cooling settings remotely. Additionally, if it's too hot or cold indoors, one may lower the heat or air conditioning or go for a walk outside. By taking these simple steps, we can help ensure that the future of utilities is bright!

© Debashish Roy 2024
D. Roy, *AI for Utilities*, https://doi.org/10.1007/979-8-8688-0202-7_2

This chapter will discuss four key themes shaping the future of utility companies. The first theme is about the sustainable planet, the second is an intelligent energy ecosystem, the third is about demand from the community and consumer, and the fourth is inventing a new business model.

Sustainable Planet

Sustainability is meeting the present generation's needs without compromising future generations' ability to meet their own needs. It is a holistic approach to development that considers human activities' economic, social, and environmental impacts. In practical terms, sustainability involves making choices and taking actions that promote economic prosperity, social well-being, and environmental protection. This can involve using resources more efficiently and responsibly, developing alternative energy sources, reducing waste, and conserving ecosystems and biodiversity.

Sustainability is important because the world faces various environmental, social, and economic challenges, including climate change, resource depletion, poverty, and inequality. We can create a more sustainable future for the planet and its inhabitants by embracing sustainability.

The need to embrace sustainability arises from various environmental, social, and economic challenges facing today's world. Some of the key reasons include

1. **Environmental degradation:** The increasing levels of greenhouse gas emissions, depletion of natural resources, and degradation of ecosystems have led to a growing concern for the planet's health.

2. **Climate change**: Climate change is one of the biggest threats facing the world today, with rising temperatures and the increasing frequency of extreme weather events.

3. **Resource depletion**: The unsustainable use of finite resources such as oil, natural gas, and minerals are leading to their depletion and the need for alternative sources of energy and materials.

4. **Economic development**: Sustainability is becoming increasingly important for economic development, as it helps to promote long-term economic growth and stability by reducing the costs associated with environmental degradation and resource depletion.

5. **Social responsibility**: Companies and organizations have a growing sense of social responsibility to minimize their environmental impact and promote sustainable development.

In summary, the need to embrace sustainability stems from the desire to address these challenges and promote a more sustainable future for both the environment and human society.

The world's population is expected to grow to 9.7 billion by 2050, which will inevitably strain the planet's resources. Sustainable technologies and practices can help preserve the planet and its resources for future generations. Sustainable products, services, and technologies are non-polluting and meet the needs of both people and the planet. Also, they can be consumed at a rate that does not exceed the Earth's capacity to regenerate. Sustainable technologies can be incorporated into new and existing products, services, and systems.

Fossil fuels such as coal, crude oil, and natural gas formed millions of years ago. Unfortunately, these fuels are non-renewable, which means they cannot be replaced once they are used.

The utility industry includes businesses that supply customers with electricity, gas, and water – essential services that are deeply intertwined with the economy. This sector is susceptible to economic changes; for instance, during economic downturns, demand for utilities may decrease as businesses scale back operations, while in times of economic growth, demand typically increases as businesses expand.

When it comes to investing in this industry, there are several avenues to consider. Investors might purchase stocks or bonds from utility companies, which are often seen as stable investments due to the essential nature of their services. Additionally, investment in infrastructure, such as upgrading the electric grid or expanding renewable energy sources, can be undertaken by private companies, public utilities, or government entities. Municipal water companies, while providing essential services, often operate as public entities rather than traditional businesses, which can affect how investments in them are structured.

As for sustainable energy, investing in renewable technologies such as solar, wind, and energy storage can help protect against the volatility of fossil fuel prices and the regulatory risks associated with carbon emissions. These investments are typically made by utility companies, private investors, or through public–private partnerships aimed at transitioning to a more sustainable energy future.

To clarify the economic changes referenced, fluctuations in energy demand, regulatory shifts, technological advancements, and the availability of resources all play roles. For example, an economic recession might lead to reduced energy consumption, affecting utility revenues, while a booming economy could increase energy demand and drive up prices. These factors underscore the importance of carefully considering the broader economic context when investing in the utility sector.

Energy Transition

The 21st century is shaping up to be very different from what we're accustomed to. The energy sector is only one of the numerous issues the globe will be dealing with that may change the path of history as we know it. The energy business is facing a future that will be substantially different from the past due to climate change and enormous growth in demand for electricity in emerging nations. In this article, we explore some of the top trends that will define the future of energy.

The world is transitioning from conventional energy sources to renewable sources. Sustainability, cost-effectiveness, and the battle against climate change are the key drivers of this transformation. Solar and wind power have been experiencing rapid growth in recent years, a trend that is expected to continue and accelerate in the upcoming years. This ongoing expansion is driven by decreasing costs, technological advancements, and increasing support from governments and private investors. As these renewable energy sources become more integrated into the global energy mix, their share of total energy production is anticipated to rise significantly. A shift toward the East is also occurring in the world's energy mix. China is emerging as a major player in the global energy market. In the upcoming years, solar and wind power are anticipated to experience substantial growth.

The unprecedented growth of renewable energy sources and the shifting energy mix will soon have a considerable impact on the demand for and supply of power. The transformation of the energy sector is expected to continue to be driven by declining costs of renewable energy, improving efficiency in the energy system, and increasing awareness of the benefits of the transformation.

Increasing awareness of climate change and the need for cleaner energy is expected to transform the energy sector.

In addition, the benefits of the transition are expected to increase awareness of the need for the transition. Increased awareness is expected to lead to increased demand for cleaner energy and, thus, an increase in the markets for cleaner energy. Further developments in energy efficiency are anticipated to result from the rising demand for cleaner energy.

The Electric Decade

From the late 19th century until the mid-20th century, electricity was produced almost exclusively by burning fossil fuels. The invention of the photovoltaic cell in 1954 marked a significant milestone in harnessing solar power. During the 1960s and 1970s, scientists and engineers focused on improving the efficiency and cost-effectiveness of these cells, aiming to develop consumer-grade and production-scale systems. By the 1980s, small-scale photovoltaic systems were beginning to be used, and by the mid-1990s, solar energy had become a more viable source of electricity, paving the way for the growth we see today. Due to technological improvements and lowering costs, solar energy is now a viable source of electricity for many of the global population. Electricity transformed the United States from an agrarian civilization to an urban and industrial one from the late 19th to the early 20th centuries. Electricity powered new manufacturing, communications, and entertainment forms and helped reduce domestic labor's burden. Electricity also transformed how people thought about and experienced the world around them.

By the 1920s, electric companies had standardized the voltage and plugs for appliances. This meant people no longer had to choose which voltage they preferred – 110 or 220.

As electricity became more standardized, it unified the country, transforming what was once a luxury into a necessity available to nearly everyone. The development of the electric grid made affordable, dependable electricity widely accessible, leading to the proliferation of home electrical appliances such as electric lighting, fans, stoves, and vacuum cleaners.

Today, the drivers of rapidly shifting demand patterns are changing again, driven by the electrification of various sectors. The push for more sustainable energy solutions is leading to the increased adoption of electric vehicles (EVs), electric stoves, heat pumps, and other electrified home systems. As consumers and industries move away from fossil fuels, the demand for electricity is expected to rise significantly. This shift is also prompting utilities to rethink grid management and capacity to ensure reliable service as demand patterns evolve.

The electrification of transportation, for instance, is poised to be one of the most significant contributors to rising electricity demand. Similarly, the adoption of electric heating and cooling systems, as well as the integration of smart technologies and energy storage solutions, are reshaping how electricity is consumed and managed in homes and businesses across the country.

Window screens, which were simpler to open and close and effectively kept out insects, increasingly replaced wooden shutters in homes. Finally, electric razors were introduced at the end of the decade, heralding the end of the daily ritual of shaving with a blade. Initially, electric razors were expensive, difficult to get, and only suitable for specific kinds of facial hair. The first electric shaver was introduced by Jacob Schick in 1931, marking a significant innovation in personal grooming technology. Schick's design was a plug-in device that revolutionized shaving by eliminating the need for traditional razors and shaving cream. It wasn't until the 1960s that Norelco (a brand of Philips) introduced the first cordless, battery-powered shaver, offering users the convenience of shaving without being tethered to an electrical outlet. This development further advanced the accessibility and ease of electric shavers, making them a staple in personal grooming.

Now that electricity technology has advanced, traditional items in our culture are becoming more electric. We are considering buying electric cars and powering many of those appliances with renewable energy. Our community and its plans will thrive in the coming decade as we switch to renewable energy sources and move away from passing to wells.

Energy Efficiency

According to the International Energy Agency, energy efficiency will significantly grow over the next ten years, substantially impacting the environment. In addition, the Paris climate agreement aims to limit global warming to 2 degrees Celsius, and research shows that the next decade will be crucial in achieving this goal.

By the end of the 2020s, energy efficiency is projected to contribute significantly to global emissions reductions, potentially accounting for one-third of the reductions needed to meet the Paris Agreement's targets. This is based on analyses from the International Energy Agency (IEA) and other research institutions, which emphasize that energy efficiency improvements across sectors such as transportation, industry, and buildings will be crucial for achieving these climate goals.

Since the early 1980s, the average efficiency of electricity usage has increased by approximately 30%, largely due to technological advancements and government regulations. Looking ahead, the average efficiency of power use is projected to increase by another 30% over the next decade, driven by continued innovation and regulatory measures. These improvements not only enhance efficiency but also have the added benefit of reducing electricity costs for consumers.

Another potential solution to climate change is the development of green artificial intelligence. AI has the potential to significantly lower manufacturing's contribution to greenhouse gas emissions. While the utilization of AI today demands significant computing resources, which in turn requires a substantial amount of electricity, the future of AI could be designed with greater efficiency in mind. As AI continues to advance, it is likely to play a crucial role in optimizing the efficiency of power grids and other energy infrastructure. The expectation is that, although AI's current electricity demands are high, the efficiency gains enabled by AI could far outweigh these costs, leading to net positive outcomes in terms of overall energy savings and improved infrastructure performance.

Intelligent Energy Ecosystem

As the world progresses, the demand for energy increases. Along with this demand comes the need for more efficient and sustainable energy sources. A network of interconnected energy sources that collaborate to meet the world's expanding energy demand will make up the intelligent energy ecosystem of the future. Various energy sources, including conventional and renewable energy sources like coal and natural gas and wind and solar, will power this ecosystem. The key to making this ecosystem work is to have a way to store and distribute the energy so that it is available when and where it is needed.

The intelligent energy ecosystem of the future will need to adapt to the world's changing needs. The ecosystem must adapt when new technologies are created and new energy demands materialize. The intelligent energy ecosystem of the future will be a critical part of the world's infrastructure. It will provide the energy to power homes, businesses, and factories. It will also help reduce the impact of climate change by providing a cleaner and more sustainable energy source.

Distributed Energy Resources

Distributed energy resources are technologies that generate power where it's needed. They can be on the grid or off. These can be solar panels, wind turbines, fuel cells, or other power-generating equipment. Grid overburden occurs when the demand on the electrical grid exceeds its capacity to deliver power reliably. This issue has become increasingly critical with the growing electrification of transportation, heating, and other sectors. As more devices and systems rely on electricity, the grid is under more pressure, leading to potential outages, inefficiencies, and the need for costly upgrades.

Power autonomy refers to the ability of individuals, communities, or businesses to generate and manage their own energy supply independently of the central grid. This can be achieved through distributed energy resources (DERs) like solar panels, wind turbines, and battery storage systems, which are located close to the point of use rather than centralized in large power plants.

Given these challenges, many experts predict that distributed energy will become a more prominent power source in the future. Distributed energy systems reduce the strain on the central grid by generating power locally and can enhance energy security, resilience, and efficiency. They also provide greater flexibility in meeting energy demand and can be crucial in managing grid overburden, particularly as the transition to renewable energy accelerates.

Any energy-producing technology not connected to the primary power grid falls under this category. They can be anything from solar panels to energy storage systems and even electric vehicle charging stations. Installing distributed energy resources frequently aims to lessen reliance on the grid and lower overall energy expenditures. While the ability to generate your power and maintain autonomy during a power outage is a significant advantage of distributed energy technologies like home solar panels and battery storage, the benefits extend far beyond that.

For consumers, distributed energy resources (DERs) such as solar panels combined with battery storage offer both supply- and demand-side benefits. On the supply side, these systems can reduce dependency on utility providers, allowing homeowners to produce their own electricity, potentially achieving a positive return on investment (ROI) over time. This is particularly true in regions where electricity rates are tiered, as consumers can optimize their energy consumption patterns to minimize costs by using stored energy during peak pricing periods.

From the utility's perspective, distributed storage systems can help smooth demand on the grid, especially during times of high energy use, such as at night when people charge electric vehicles (EVs). These systems can be crucial in managing demand when renewable energy sources like solar power are not available, thus helping to stabilize the grid. Moreover, DERs can provide utilities with greater flexibility in managing supply and demand, contributing to overall grid reliability and efficiency.

However, there are also trade-offs to consider. For instance, the widespread adoption of DERs could lead to challenges in grid management, such as ensuring balanced load distribution and maintaining the stability of voltage and frequency across the network. Additionally, while DERs can reduce costs for consumers, they might also necessitate investments in infrastructure upgrades and new technologies by utilities, which could be passed on to customers.

What Is an Intelligent Grid?

The term "intelligent grid" refers to the advanced technologies that enable the development of a smart grid. While the smart grid itself is a modernized electrical grid that uses digital technology to improve reliability, efficiency, and sustainability, the intelligent grid takes this a step further by incorporating highly automated, self-regulating systems that gather data and use it to make real-time decisions.

The primary distinction between a smart grid and an intelligent grid lies in the latter's autonomous, adaptable, and self-learning capabilities. While both grids use advanced technology to monitor and manage energy distribution, the intelligent grid can autonomously adjust to changes in supply and demand, optimize performance, and even learn from past data to improve future operations. In essence, the intelligent grid represents the next evolution of the smart grid, with enhanced capabilities for automation, adaptability, and decision-making.

The Intelligent grid is the future of electric power distribution. It is a system that uses information and communication technologies to gather and analyze data about the electricity system and then make decisions about how to operate it to improve its performance.

What Is the Goal Behind Creating an Intelligent Grid?

An intelligent grid aims to make the electricity system more reliable, efficient, and sustainable. For example, an intelligent grid can help utilities avoid blackouts, restore power faster after outages, and integrate renewable energy sources into the grid.

What Are the Components of an Intelligent Grid?

An intelligent grid comprises many components, including smart meters, sensors, and advanced software. Smart meters measure the electricity a customer uses and then send that information back to the utility.

Additionally, sensors measure various aspects of the electric grid, such as voltage, current, and temperature. Advanced software is used to analyze the smart meters and sensors data to make decisions about how to operate the grid.

What Are the Benefits of an Intelligent Grid?

The benefits of an intelligent grid include improved reliability, efficiency, and sustainability. An intelligent grid can help utilities avoid blackouts, restore power faster after outages, and integrate renewable energy sources into the grid. In simple terms, the future grid will be like a networked computer system that uses software, sensors, and artificial intelligence to regulate the flow of electricity.

What Is the Difference Between a Smart Grid and an Intelligent Grid?

The smart grid is a system that collects data and works to balance the electricity supply and demand. On the other hand, the intelligent grid is a system that actively responds to changes in the electricity grid to avoid or reduce the need for grid balancing. The ability of the intelligent grid to self-heal and actively react to changes in the electrical grid is the primary distinction between the intelligent and the smart grid. In other words, the intelligent grid is designed to avoid the need for grid balancing.

This difference may seem subtle, but it's a crucial distinction. With the smart grid, grid operators must step in when the system needs balancing. This necessitates more time and money. Additionally, it makes blackouts more likely. Grid operators no longer need to intervene, thanks to the intelligent grid. A two-way communication technology called the intelligent grid gives users more control over how and when power is delivered. The system enables utilities to monitor and remotely control electricity demand, gather consumer usage information, and evaluate the likelihood of energy shortages at various times of the day. It also enables customers to manage their energy use and receive real-time feedback about their power usage during different times of the day, allowing them to cut back on unnecessary usage during peak times.

The grid is evolving into what's known as "the intelligent grid." This transformation occurs as the grid connects with an increasing number of intelligent devices that can exchange data and communicate with one another. The grid is becoming more dynamic and adaptive due to the increased connection, and it can now be managed by software. Grid edge devices – such as solar panels, electric vehicles, and battery storage systems – are increasingly capable of responding to changing conditions. The grid becomes a network when more and more devices can communicate with one another, creating new opportunities. AI will power the future intelligent grid. Moving away from the smart grid and building the new intelligent grid is the way to go.

Connected Microgrid

The world has seen a spike in the number of natural disasters and power outages in the recent past. Storms, floods, and droughts are becoming worse and more frequent because of climate change. This puts millions of lives at risk and causes billions in damage. Interconnected microgrids can help in reducing these vulnerabilities. During power outages, they enable communities to keep their lights on. When there are blackouts, they offer a backup power source. They allow communities to rely less on centralized power networks and change over to distributed energy systems.

Microgrids are grids comprising several small energy sources, such as solar panels, battery packs, and small-scale wind turbines. They can be connected to the traditional grid or operate independently of it. As the world switches to cleaner energy sources, their importance is growing. In a microgrid, electricity can be generated in real-time to fulfill the demands of the system's users from a variety of small units, such as rooftop solar panels. Some microgrids are designed to function as self-sufficient energy systems that can keep critical loads operating in the event of an outage on the main grid.

We may anticipate increased microgrid development soon as cities and countries look to lessen their reliance on centralized power plants. Additionally, we can anticipate the development of "virtual power plants," which are microgrids built to work in tandem to ensure that the system has adequate generating capacity to satisfy consumers' demands.

Community and Consumer

What Is a CCA?

A Community Choice Aggregator (CCA) is a local government entity that aggregates the electric energy requirements of its residential and commercial customers to secure lower-cost, cleaner energy supplies from energy service providers (ESPs).

How Does CCA Operate?

CCAs are created through legislation at the state level and are thus far only operational in California. To become a CCA, a city or county must first express interest to their state's energy commission. Once the state commission approves the formation of the CCA, the local government needs to develop an implementation plan.

The first step of this plan is to develop the CCA's governing board, which is typically made up of representatives from the local community. Once the board is in place, the CCA can develop its energy generation plans or procure energy from ESPs.

What Are the Benefits of CCA?

CCAs provide their communities with several advantages. Because CCAs can aggregate their customers' energy needs, they can negotiate for lower energy rates. Additionally, CCAs can obtain their energy from more sustainable, renewable sources. This can help to reduce the community's carbon footprint and improve local air quality.

CCAs also offer customers more choices and control over their energy service. Customers can opt out of the CCA service, but they will still benefit from the company's reduced energy prices. In addition, customers can participate in the CCA's demand response programs, which can further lower their energy costs. Since the creation of CCAs is a recent development in the energy sector, several issues must be resolved. One of the biggest challenges is ensuring the CCA has enough customers to negotiate competitive energy rates. Another challenge is ensuring that the CCA has the financial and technical resources necessary to implement its plans.

Despite these challenges, CCAs offer a unique opportunity for communities to take control of their energy future. By cooperating, communities may achieve more affordable, environmentally friendly energy sources to benefit all locals.

Evolving Regulation

The electricity industry is constantly evolving, and so is the regulation surrounding it. This transition is fueled by several variables, including technological advancements, modifications to how power is produced and used, and the emergence of new market competitors.

The laws that control the industry must change as the industry itself does. Many players, from government organizations to business entities, are competing for a role in how the energy sector is governed in this complex and dynamic environment. There are considerable key issues currently being debated when it comes to regulating the electricity industry. These include the role of renewable energy, the future of coal-fired power plants, and the role of new technologies like battery storage.

As more nations seek to lessen their dependency on fossil fuels, renewable energy is becoming more and more significant in the electricity sector. This has led to a debate about the role of renewable energy in the electricity sector and how it should be regulated.

Coal-fired power plants are a significant source of greenhouse gas emissions, and there is an ongoing debate about whether they should be phased out. This is a complicated problem; many entities are involved, from government organizations to business leaders.

The rise of new technologies, like battery storage, is also changing the landscape of the electricity sector. As a result, there is a discussion regarding how these technologies should be regulated because they are frequently not fully understood.

From Consumer to Prosumers

A prosumer is someone who both consumes and produces a good or service. Most individuals used to be consumers who exclusively used their utility providers to buy power. However, as solar energy and other renewable energy sources gain popularity, more people are becoming prosumers who produce their electricity and sell it back to the grid. There are many benefits to becoming a prosumer. First, it can save you money on your electricity bill. You can make money by selling the extra electricity you produce back to the grid if you produce more than you need. Second, it can help to increase the stability of the grid. Large, centralized electricity plants are not as necessary when there are more prosumers. This can lead to a more robust and reliable electricity grid.

Finally, it can help to reduce your carbon footprint. Because solar energy and other renewable energy sources emit relatively little carbon dioxide into the atmosphere, producing electricity can help you reduce environmental impact. If you are interested in becoming a prosumer, there are a few things you need to do. First, you need to install solar panels or another form of renewable energy generation. Second, you need to purchase a net meter from your utility provider. This will allow you to sell any excess electricity you generate back to the grid. To reduce your electricity use, you must be sure that you are employing energy-efficient activities and appliances in your home. The transition from electricity consumer to prosumer is a great way to save money, help the environment, and increase the grid's stability. If you want to become a prosumer, start by installing solar panels and purchasing a net meter.

Eliminating Energy Poverty

Energy poverty is a pressing global issue that needs to be addressed. It is defined as the lack of access to clean, affordable energy. This means that many people do not have access to the electricity they need to power their homes and their lives.

Energy poverty is a significant problem because it is one factor keeping people trapped in a cycle of poverty. It is hard to escape poverty if you cannot even afford to pay for basic needs like electricity. Energy poverty also has a huge impact on health. People who do not have access to clean energy are more likely to get sick and die from preventable diseases.

There are many ways to eliminate energy poverty. One way is to provide access to clean, affordable energy. This can be done through initiatives like solar power or wind power. Helping people reduce their energy costs is another strategy to end energy poverty. This can be accomplished by offering incentives for energy-saving appliances or by implementing energy efficiency initiatives. It is important to note that energy poverty is a worldwide problem, not just for developing countries. It is also a problem in developed countries like the United States. Many people in the United States cannot afford to pay their energy bills. This is why it is important for developed countries to also take action to eliminate energy poverty.

There are many ways to eliminate energy poverty. However, it is an important issue that needs to be addressed.

Inventing New Business Models

The recent rise in population, industrialization, and other factors have contributed to increased energy demand, which, when coupled with rapid expansion in distributed energy sources and renewable energy, means the utility industry has to evolve and adapt. Creating new business models that are more effective and efficient than existing ones is one method to do this. This can be done by studying the current models and looking for ways to improve them.

Some of the most successful business models in the utility industry are the ones that focus on customer service and satisfaction. Others have been able to reduce costs by implementing new technologies. At the same time, some others have succeeded in raising profits by developing fresh strategies for advertising their products. Whatever the situation, it is obvious that the utility sector has a lot of room for innovation. Utilities must continuously search for fresh approaches to enhance their business models if they are to succeed. They must also be willing to take risks and experiment with new ideas. Only by doing this will they be able to stay ahead of the curve and remain successful in an ever-changing industry.

Energy As a Service

Energy-as-a-service (EaaS) refers to a new business model in which energy is provided as a service rather than a product. In this model, customers pay for energy use rather than for the purchase of energy products. Energy-as-a-service (EaaS) is a business concept in which clients pay for an energy service without making any initial capital investment. EaaS models typically take the form of a subscription for a service company's electrical devices or control of energy usage to supply the desired energy service.

The EaaS model has emerged in response to the growing need for cleaner, more sustainable energy sources. The conventional energy business model is no longer viable as the globe switches from fossil fuels to renewable energy. With the EaaS paradigm, energy suppliers may give their clients affordable access to clean, sustainable energy. Many companies, including Google and Microsoft, have already adopted the EaaS model. These companies have invested in clean energy projects, such as wind and solar farms, and then sell the energy they produce to their customers.

The EaaS model has various benefits for both energy providers and consumers. It enables energy providers to access a new source of income. It makes clean, sustainable energy more affordable for customers. The EaaS model is still in its early stages, and it remains to be seen how it will evolve. However, it can fundamentally alter the energy sector and give everyone access to a more sustainable and reasonable future.

Energy Marketplace

In the future, the energy marketplace will be very different from today's. Many new energy sources will be available, and buying and selling energy will be done more flexibly. One of the big changes will be the emergence of new energy sources, such as solar, wind, and geothermal. These renewable sources will make up a much larger share of the energy mix as they become more cost-competitive with traditional sources like coal and natural gas.

Another change will be the way that energy is bought and sold. Most energy is currently sold through long-term contracts, but the energy market will be much more flexible. Consumers will be able to choose from a variety of energy providers and purchase energy in real time based on their needs.

The future energy marketplace will be more dynamic and flexible, giving consumers more choice and control over their energy use.

Microgrid As a Service

Microgrid-as-a-Service (MaaS) is a new business model for deploying microgrids. In this model, a microgrid operator or developer offers a customer a microgrid solution as a service rather than a tangible good. The customer pays for the service, typically monthly, and the microgrid developer or operator is responsible for the microgrid's performance.

Customers can benefit from the microgrid-as-a-service concept in several ways. First, it reduces the up-front cost of deploying a microgrid by eliminating the need to purchase equipment. Second, it provides a lower overall cost of ownership since the microgrid developer or operator is responsible for the maintenance and operation of the microgrid. Third, it offers customers flexibility regarding how much they use the microgrid – they can pay for only the electricity they use rather than purchasing a fixed amount of capacity.

Since it offers a new revenue source and a method to distinguish their microgrid solutions, the microgrid-as-a-service model also appeals to developers and operators. In addition, under this model, developers and operators can better manage the risk associated with deploying a microgrid since they are not responsible for the entire project.

The microgrid-as-a-service model is still in its early stages, and several challenges need to be addressed before it can be widely adopted. First, the business model needs to be proven – many pilot projects are underway, but it will take time to see whether they are successful. Second, the regulatory environment needs to be clarified – currently, there is no clear regulatory framework for microgrids in many jurisdictions. Third, financing needs to be put in place to support the development of microgrids-as-a-service.

Despite these challenges, the microgrid-as-a-service model has the potential to revolutionize the way microgrids are deployed. Furthermore, by making microgrids more accessible and affordable, this model could help to accelerate the transition to a clean energy future.

Due to the rising need for convenient and sustainable transportation options, the MaaS concept, which combines numerous forms of transportation into a single, helpful service, has recently gained a lot of attention. According to a report by MarketsandMarkets, the global MaaS market is expected to reach $1005.8 billion by 2030, growing at a compound annual growth rate of 23.5% from 2021 to 2030.

Several factors, including the increasing adoption of electric and autonomous vehicles, the rise of shared mobility services, and the growing demand for sustainable transportation options, are driving the growth of the MaaS market. In addition, because of their rapidly urbanizing populations, nations like China and India, undergoing significant industrial expansion, are anticipated to fuel the need for MaaS. According to the EIA (Energy Information Administration), India and China will account for half of the world's total increase in energy consumption by 2040. This industrial development is propelling the global energy industry and boosting the microgrid demand.

Connected Energy Services

In the future, energy services will be more connected than ever before. This will allow for more efficient use of resources and improved coordination between energy service providers.

One example of a connected energy service is a smart grid. A smart grid is an electricity network that uses digital technology to deliver electricity more efficiently and reliably. It also enables two-way communication between the electricity provider and the customer. As a result, customers can receive advice on saving energy and real-time information about how much energy they use. Another example of a connected energy service is a demand response system. Using financial incentives to encourage consumers to use less energy during peak demand periods, this approach aids in managing the electricity demand. This can help to avoid blackouts and reduce the need for expensive new power plants.

The future of energy services will likely be more connected, efficient, and responsive to customer needs. This will help to create a more sustainable and affordable energy system.

Key Takeaways

- Utilities will play a critical role in making our planet sustainable by providing clean energy, water, and waste management solutions.

- The Intelligent Energy Ecosystem would be powered by various energy sources, including renewable sources such as solar and wind power. Additionally, it would leverage already-built energy infrastructure, including the electrical grid. The ecosystem would be designed to be flexible and adaptable so that it could respond to changes in energy demand and supply.

- Several community and consumer groups actively promote renewable energy and energy efficiency, and some are working to develop new business models for community-owned renewable energy. These groups can be important partners for utilities in developing and implementing new business models.

- As consumers become less loyal to the traditional utility model and establish more direct connections with power producers in the form of solar, wind, and other distributed generation, utilities will have to adapt to keep up with the times.

CHAPTER 3

Utilities Building Digital DNA

As technology advances and the digital landscape continues to evolve; utilities must adapt to remain competitive and secure. To succeed in this rapidly changing environment, many utilities are turning to the concept of building Digital DNA – a set of strategic objectives that can be used to improve their operations and increase customer satisfaction. This chapter will provide a comprehensive overview of Digital DNA, exploring its core elements and the benefits it can bring to utilities. It will also introduce the key strategies and tools utilities can use to implement Digital DNA and the challenges they may face along the way. Finally, it will discuss how Digital DNA can be used to create a more secure and reliable utility for customers. By the end of this chapter, readers will have a better understanding of what Digital DNA is and how it can help utilities to better serve their customers.

Digital DNA

Our DNA contains the information that characterizes our life and tells the tale of it. This is an important element of any progress. Utility companies are undergoing a significant transformation, and to succeed on this path, their DNA must be changed to resemble oil. To change one's DNA, one must abandon one's old ways of thinking and adopt new ones. Hence, rebuilding the legacy infrastructure, upskilling its people, migrating to the

© Debashish Roy 2024
D. Roy, *AI for Utilities*, https://doi.org/10.1007/979-8-8688-0202-7_3

cloud, and many more. This is not a destination; it's a journey that needs to be started as soon as possible if the utility company wants to be relevant in the future. Building utilities of the future requires rebuilding its DNA with digital technologies. I'll talk about some of the critical elements of this digital DNA in this chapter.

Cloud Continuum for Utilities

Adoption for utility companies brings many benefits, such as improved operational efficiency, increased data security, real-time monitoring, and reduced costs.

With the steady acceptance of infrastructure and software solutions, many utilities have already started their cloud journey. However, creating a corporate cloud strategy has proven challenging. Those obstacles, however, are surmountable. Concerns about security, data, and control are largely figments of the past. A comprehensive strategy that integrates new technology with the new working practices that cloud computing offers to the company is necessary to attain value. Moreover, the cloud may be at the heart of raising utilities to a bigger role, speeding energy transformation, and meeting corporate sustainability goals.

IT operational paradigms in utilities are under pressure to undergo a drastic transformation.

COVID-19 has heightened the importance of the utility cloud imperative. As utilities attempted to manage uncertainty and migrate to a different operating model, the scalability, resilience, flexibility, and accessibility of the public cloud became far more appealing in weeks.

The utility executives evaluate the prospective new landscape and monitor the public cloud's outstanding performance in recent months to determine when to scale up their utility enterprise cloud plan. One of the main drivers of AI adoption in the utility sector will be the cloud.

Cloud Strategy

Cloud investments deliver results. However, realizing the full advantage of cloud computing might be tricky. Utilities must have a clearly defined strategy if they want to fully grasp the value of the cloud. Cloud strategy can be seen as a process or a series of necessary steps to achieve your desired results. It can be a simple process or a detailed plan of action to get to your desired destination. A cloud strategy is a practical guide that can be used by businesses and individuals to make the most of cloud technologies.

The following are the primary steps in creating a cloud strategy. First, assess your current situation – what are your business or organization's current problems and issues? What are the main goals that you want to achieve? Next, define your target – what is the desired outcome or result you want? Next, decide on a cloud approach – what approach should you take to achieve your goals? What technologies should be used? Finally, implement the strategy – what steps should be taken to implement the plan?

To ensure your company thrives in a cloud-based world, you must develop a strategic approach to cloud adoption. By adhering to these five essential components, you can develop an enterprise-grade cloud strategy that offers genuine value to your company:

1. **Assess your organization's readiness for cloud computing.** There is no defined "right" time to make the switch, but a few things to consider before you leap.

2. **Define your goals for the cloud.** Because each cloud implementation is unique, you should choose what you want to achieve before you begin.

3. **Research vendors and select a partner.** You'll need something to jump-start your migration, so you can't just dive in headfirst.

41

4. **Create a detailed plan.** You can't just make this switch without a plan in place. You will want a detailed plan to ensure everything is covered.

5. **Communicate your plan, goals, and vendor selection to your team.** You don't want people caught off guard when the switch happens.

Modernizing Decade-Old Infrastructure

A few advantages of cloud computing for utility organizations include agility, scalability, and cost savings. However, most of the software used by utilities companies is over ten years old. It's usually written in a programming language that the vendor no longer supports.

Upscaling your data centers with cloud technologies like server virtualization, containers, open source software, and artificial intelligence (AI) can help companies improve their operational efficiency, cut costs, and reduce the risk of outages. These technologies allow companies to transfer their data from on-site data centers to the cloud. Companies that use the cloud can scale their resources up or down as needed. They also receive regular updates and patches to protect their data and applications from cyber threats.

Develop Cloud Talent

Any company's growth and development depend on hiring new talent, but in cloud computing, it is more crucial because success depends on a team with specialized knowledge and expertise. A company can implement various practices to grow its talent and improve its hiring processes to acquire the best staff possible. The cloud offers utility companies many advantages but also presents some challenges. Finding and nurturing the talent the sector needs to compete in the digital age is one of the significant problems.

The utility industry has traditionally been a laggard in adopting new technologies. This has led to a lack of technical expertise within the industry. However, as the industry looks to the cloud to support its digital transformation, it enables new business or operating models, helps new entrants disrupt the sector, and empowers incumbents to reach new performance levels.

There are several ways in which utility companies can develop cloud talent. One of the most effective methods is to partner with educational institutions that offer cloud-related courses and programs. By partnering with these institutions, utility companies can ensure their employees have the necessary skills and knowledge to support digital transformation of the industry.

Investing in internal training and development initiatives is another option for utility businesses to cultivate cloud expertise. These programs can help employees to gain the skills and knowledge they need to support the industry's digital transformation.

Finally, utility companies can also look to external sources to help them develop cloud talent. The sector's digital transformation can be supported by several businesses that provide cloud-related services. Utility firms can collaborate with these businesses to obtain access to the expertise and assets necessary to compete in the digital era.

Re-invent Your Legacy Applications

Businesses that are prepared to invest more time and money in their cloud migration may see it as a chance to update and enhance the architecture of their applications. These companies can use one of two broad strategies. The first technique is a sort of medium ground. Businesses must identify key aspects of their software incompatible with the cloud hosting provider and provide enough resources to optimize those areas to fully profit from cloud computing. There are no fundamental changes, only optimizations. The freshly improved program is then moved to the cloud hosting service.

This strategy is more expensive than the traditional lift-and-shift method, but it removes the more significant inefficiencies that might occur from just rehosting your application.

The second strategy is opposed to the lift-and-shift method. Instead, businesses must rethink, rebuild, and rearchitect their applications to effectively use cloud-native capabilities. Similarly to the previous way, the organization initially identifies areas where their application might benefit from cloud hosting services. Still, unlike the prior method, these areas can be more extensive in scope and encompass fundamental functionality.

During this stage, they may discover that just one-third of their architecture needs restructuring. They may also understand that almost all of it does. They then assign sufficient resources to carry out the refactor. This method necessitates the greatest up-front time and money due to the possibly vast scale of the project. However, for some businesses, it might result in lower ongoing costs, resulting in long-term financial savings.

For example, if an application utilizes logic that takes a significant number of resources to process and stores its data, transferring the program to the cloud with that logic intact might cost the company a lot of money.

The cloud hosting service frequently provides a more efficient solution for an application to achieve the same goal. A company loses a substantial sum of money each month if it does not redesign its program to adopt that more effective method. Most cloud hosting systems have to scale functionalities; thus, if an application is already completely compatible with the cloud hosting platform, growing swiftly while retaining application quality should be straightforward.

Data As Electricity

Data is the new electricity and is being generated in more significant quantities than ever before. Due to technological advancements, businesses and consumers are collecting and storing data at unprecedented levels, and the growth rate shows no signs of slowing. Unfortunately, data is not a utility we can turn on when needed. There is no data switch to be flipped. As a result, just like managing their physical assets, businesses and government organizations must think carefully about managing their data assets. Data is the fuel that powers AI, and utilities are no exception. In the utility sector, artificial intelligence (AI) and machine learning evaluate data from meters to maximize energy efficiency and save customer costs. In addition, AI can predict equipment failure and maintenance needs. It can also be applied to data from weather forecasting models to determine the best operating settings for the utility company's power plants.

Many industries use it to increase operational effectiveness, cut costs, and open new business models. For example, data is used in the energy industry for various purposes, including smart grids, energy storage, smart appliances, and energy management systems. Data is increasingly becoming a critical input to energy systems and processes, playing a pivotal role in shaping the future of energy. Utilities are trying to develop their data strategy, which will be essential to their digital DNA.

Building a New Data Foundation

As the world becomes increasingly connected, the volume and variety of data generated by sensors and devices only grow. From smart grids to connected homes, data is being generated, collected, and stored in significantly greater quantities and at increasing velocity, creating a data deluge. In the age of big data, organizations, governments, and people must be able to interpret data sets and transform them into useful information. There is a wide range of potential applications for data analytics in the utility industry, from managing demand to improving reliability and creating new customer offerings. However, to make the most of data, utilities must be able to trust their data.

A new generation of products and services that improve people's decision-making around their energy consumption is built on data. For example, utilities can use data to help customers save money on their bills and keep their homes warm during the chilly winter. And by tracking performance and identifying issues before they result in outages, data may also assist utilities in keeping their systems operating as efficiently as possible.

Smart meters generate huge amounts of data, but just having data is not enough. You need the right data at the right time to drive your business forward. So, you need a data foundation that can collect, store, process, and make sense of data from any device, format, or scale.

Data As a Service

Given the increasing global adoption of distributed and decentralized energy resources like solar and wind, a new level of communication and data management across all energy stakeholders will be necessary. We are witnessing the quick development of data-driven energy technology, which will necessitate greater data literacy and transparency from utilities, regulators, consumers, and other stakeholders in the energy ecosystem. Providing a common framework for data exchange, data integrity, and interoperability will be essential to the energy ecosystem.

Data can be the basis for new services that improve the efficiency of utility companies and their customers. For example, data from sensors on smart meters can be analyzed to predict power outages, track equipment maintenance needs, or remotely monitor the health of utility employees. Customers can benefit from data-driven services such as usage-based rate plans or products that offer incentives for energy conservation. Data-driven services require trust, which is greatly enhanced by adopting data standards.

Data is the new oilO, and utilities are the perfect example. Smart grids, the Internet of Things (IoT), and other technologies that collect data can be immensely valuable and only increase in value. Data is what powers the machine-to-machine communication that enables smart grids, and data is vital to the analysis that determines the ideal settings of each machine. Therefore, utilities have an excellent reason to collect data and can monetize it by hosting it in the cloud.

Monetizing Data

Data has a monetary value, especially in the utility industry. It can be used to improve operational efficiency and save money. Additionally, it can be utilized for data-driven marketing initiatives like focused energy efficiency campaigns. Utilities have an intimate understanding of their customers' energy usage patterns, which can be used to tailor marketing campaigns. For example, an electric utility company may sell a program for customers to install energy-efficient LED lighting in their homes. Since the utility company has access to information about the power usage of each home, it can create a marketing campaign to reach out to customers who generally use more power during certain hours.

Data can be the basis for new services that improve the efficiency of utility companies and their customers. For example, data from sensors on smart meters can be analyzed to predict power outages, track equipment maintenance needs, or remotely monitor the health of utility employees. Data-driven services like usage-based pricing plans or goods that provide energy-saving incentives might benefit customers. Data-driven services require trust, which is greatly enhanced by adopting data standards.

Data-driven utilities collect data at every stage of the electricity consumption: generation, transmission, distribution, consumption, and even at consumption endpoint. This data can be monetized by offering it to a third-party service provider, who can analyze it and provide value-added services. For example, an energy management system collects all data about the consumption and usage of electricity, which are then sold to third-party clients.

Intelligent Enterprise

Utilities' Strategic Priorities Focus on Operating as Intelligent, Sustainable Enterprises to Drive Innovation and Resilience in the Energy Sector. Innovative utility companies successfully operate within their traditional business model of producing, delivering, and selling energy while looking for new income sources and business outcomes. The following success methods demonstrate various techniques based on the evolution of existing goods and processes and the exploration of disruptive new business models. Transforming the ERP code is essential for evolving as an intelligent enterprise. Transformation involves three main elements discussed below:

Transform the Core

The transformation of the core business systems like ERP (enterprise resource planning refers to software organizations' use to manage day-to-day business activities such as accounting, procurement, project management, risk management and compliance, and supply chain operations) can help utilities to become more efficient and customer-focused. Some of the main benefits of transforming the core business systems can be improved operational efficiency: operational efficiency is the main goal of ERP implementation. By automating daily tasks, lowering human labor and mistake rates, increasing information visibility, etc., ERP deployment will enhance operational efficiency. Visibility of information: ERP will help increase information visibility to various stakeholders. Ease of doing business: ERP implementation will make it easy to do business with the utility company. Investment protection: ERP implementation will also help increase investment protection by reducing the risk of obsolescence.

Secure Your Footprint

To safeguard your brand and company from online dangers, securing your ERP footprint is crucial. In addition, ERP is an essential component of your company's infrastructure; keeping it safe should be one of your top priorities. ERP software manages the flow of data that keeps your business running, such as purchasing, inventory, and shipping.

Utility companies carefully monitor usage and load patterns, and they can detect a sudden increase in load on a network that indicates a possible data breach. They can shut down the network to protect their customers if they detect an unauthorized load. That's bad news for your company if it cannot access important data during that time. This is where an ERP solution comes into play. If your company uses an ERP system to track and manage its data, it can set up rules that will cause the system to shut down the network if it detects a sudden spike in load. When you consider the possible consequences of a data breach, it may be worth a few hours of employee downtime.

Embrace Applied Intelligence

Enterprises are driven to innovate and expand using social, mobile, analytics, cloud, and artificial intelligence (AI) technologies. More and more enterprises are using these technologies. When starting with the customer interface, such as a mobile app or web self-service portal, it is also important to redesign core processes. Companies increasingly recognize that overhauling their core processes is as (if not more) important than overhauling their core, which is often made up of enterprise resource planning (ERP) applications deployed in the 1980s or 1990s. Every user interface and business process requires data from this core source. Embracing applied intelligence in the enterprise code is essential for evolving as an innovative utility company.

Intelligent Operation

Intelligent operation of the grid has the potential to create significant value for the electricity system, helping to support the stability of the grid and the delivery of reliable power to customers. In addition, it enables utilities to reduce operating costs by optimizing their use of assets, such as generating units, power plants, and transmission lines. The intelligent operation can be achieved by adopting various technologies, such as smart meters, data analytics, and distributed generation and automation technologies.

Automate at Scale

Enterprise-wide automation cannot be accomplished by a haphazard assembly of citizen coders or several departmental teams experimenting with a range of automation techniques. Instead, to achieve top-line growth or bottom-line performance through scale automation, companies must invest in skills, organizational structure, and technology.

Automation at scale refers to a company's ability to obtain tangible business benefits from applying automation technology to the smallest task in a single department and the largest processes across the firm. Unfortunately, the promises of automation vendors frequently hypnotize IT and business leaders, leading them to concentrate on choosing specific tools at the start of their automation initiatives while ignoring or postponing investments in the crucial organizational structures and skills needed to realize strategic business benefits.

A haphazard mixture of citizen developers or a piecemeal accumulation of departments experimenting with various automation tools cannot achieve enterprise-wide automation. To drive top-line growth or bottom-line performance via automation at scale, companies must invest in the following skills, organizational structure and technology.

Site Reliability Engineering

Site reliability engineering (SRE) is a software engineering branch that focuses on maintaining high reliability in hosted software systems. Standardization and automation are two important components of the SRE model because they help ensure reliability and scalability of systems and services. SRE combines engineering best practices, processes, and people focused on reliability. To satisfy customer expectations and maintain high dependability despite any unforeseen load or other stressors, software systems must be designed and operated with this goal in mind. The site reliability engineering practice will be very important for utility companies to evolve as modern power supplier. Site reliability engineering is vital for managing the current applications that utilities will build using cloud, data and AI.

SRE helps teams balance releasing new features and ensuring reliability by using a data-driven, reliability-focused approach to software development and operations and continuously monitoring and improving the reliability of systems and services.

1. **Reliability-focused**: SRE teams prioritize reliability and stability over the release of new features, ensuring that systems and services are designed, built, and operated with a focus on minimizing downtime and ensuring high availability.

2. **Data-driven**: SRE teams use data and metrics to inform their decisions and continuously improve the reliability of systems and services. This helps to identify and resolve issues more quickly and make informed decisions about balancing the release of new features with the need for reliability.

3. **Collaboration**: SRE teams work closely with development teams to ensure that new features are designed and implemented in a way that does not compromise reliability. This helps to ensure that the release of new features is aligned with the overall goals of the organization.

4. **Continuous improvement**: SRE teams continuously monitor and improve the reliability of systems and services, using data and metrics to inform their decisions and make improvements over time. This helps to maintain the balance between releasing new features and ensuring reliability over time.

Operational Analytics

Operational analytics is collecting and using data from your systems to make better business decisions. It applies to almost all business sectors and job functions, from supply chain management to public safety. The data that's being collected can be anything from system performance metrics to event logs. Operational analytics is commonly used for process optimization, compliance, anomaly detection, and real-time analysis.

The New IT Operating Model

The modern utility industry is under pressure like never before. New technologies are changing how energy is produced, distributed, and consumed while raising consumer expectations. This results in a perfect storm of change for utilities, and they must adapt or risk being left behind.

Fortunately, a new operating model is gaining traction in the industry, and it holds the promise of helping utilities survive and thrive in this new era. This model is known as the New IT Operating Model, and it is based on four key pillars:

1. **Cloud-First:** The New IT Operating Model is built on a cloud-first philosophy. All new applications and services will be designed for the cloud from the ground up. This will allow utilities to take advantage of the many benefits that the cloud offers, such as scalability, flexibility, and cost savings.

2. **Agile and DevOps:** The New IT Operating Model is also built on an agile and DevOps approach. This means new applications and services will be developed iteratively and incrementally, focusing on speed and agility. This will allow utilities to respond rapidly to changing customer needs and market conditions.

3. **Data-Driven:** The New IT Operating Model is also data-driven. This means that all decisions will be based on data and analytics. This will allow utilities to make better decisions about where to invest their resources and how to optimize their operations.

4. **Customer-centric:** The New IT Operating Model is also customer-centric. This means that all decisions and actions will be taken with the customer in mind. This will allow utilities to improve customer satisfaction and loyalty.

The New IT Operating Model is not a silver bullet but offers a path forward for utilities looking to survive and thrive in the new era. The New IT Operating Model is worth considering if your utility is looking to adapt to the changing landscape.

Embrace Agility

Utility companies have historically been more safety-focused and resistant to change. Many utilities have a fortress mindset that prevents fresh ideas from being implemented. Companies still rely on conventional (and usually one-dimensional) methods of getting market intelligence since their infrastructure is frequently undeveloped in the age of information networks and crowdsourcing. It may be easier for a company to implement agile software development if it is accustomed to traditional development. It may appear chaotic or out of control, yet this is not the case. It's a different style of thinking that enables a team to respond to rapidly changing needs while still delivering functional software throughout the process.

Early client involvement, quick feedback loops, and iteration contribute to agile development's ability to produce more reliable and superior products. In addition, it enables the product to adapt swiftly and efficiently to changing requirements to stay ahead of the industry's needs. Consequently, utilities gain from having instant access to new features and increased functionality.

While agile software development is not a panacea, it can better position utilities to capitalize on future software developments like machine learning, artificial intelligence, and even virtual reality. In the world of software and technology, the only constant is change. In addition to providing what utilities currently require, Clean Power Research also gives them the flexibility to satisfy rising energy-related demand in the future. Utilities may benefit from AI by automating repetitive, high-volume processes, allowing project analytics for estimation and risk prediction, generating actionable suggestions, and even making judgments.

AI has the potential to revolutionize agile development by accelerating productivity and increasing project success rates. AI technology can be used to assist in the management of agile projects. Embracing agility can assist utilities in shifting because their company changes quickly, and stop ports adapt swiftly to changing customer demands. Artificial intelligence will play an important role in this journey.

Talent Transformation

A utility can only go far with its technology, infrastructure, and service investments. True and lasting transformation is only possible with organizational agility, employee expertise, innovation, and creativity. As the power and utilities (P&U) industry transitions to a decarbonized, digital, and decentralized future, organizations compete for the talent required to drive business change and foster collaborative cultures capable of thriving in a more complex, competitive market. This talent war is a huge challenge.

Various factors shape the future of utilities, and there is no one formula for success. Additional hurdles are created by societal developments connected to the future of work, such as a generational shift in the workforce and the influence of digitalization and automation on jobs. In addition, the emergence of environmental, social, and governance (ESG) investment and new Securities and Exchange Commission rules for human capital disclosure bring new obligations and a greater need for openness.

Human capital management and culture are at the forefront of corporate governance concerns and the keys to generating long-term value for all stakeholders as the industry seeks to address the difficulties of today's changing economy.

GENERATION	TRANSMISSION	DISTRIBUTION	RETAIL
• Intelligent Planners	• 5G Network Specialist	• Cloud Architects	• Remote Call center Technologist
• Battery Engineer	• Super IoT Engineer	• Data Scientist	• Metaverse Specialist
• Automation	• Remote Monitoring Technologist	• Microgrid Engineers	• Cloud Engineers
• Cybersecurity		• Market Operation Specialist	• EV Experts
• Renewable Experts	• Space Technologist	• Enterprise Platform Engineer	• Data Privacy Specialist
• Geoscientist	• AI Engineer		• Data Analytics Engineer
• AI Engineer			• AR/VR Engineer

EMERGING TALENT NEEDS

Intelligence will be embedded in everything utilities will do in the future. The utility industry's entire value chain would require engineers' expertise in AI, machine learning, and data analytics. Tech skills also need to democratize business roles as well. Intelligence will automate and augment many traditional human-focused roles in the utility industry. Human+Machine working together would be the foundation of future talent.

Human+Machine – Augment Human Talent

There is a phenomenon in robotics and artificial intelligence called the "uncanny valley." This phenomenon describes the discomfort or revulsion some people experience when encountering a machine that is almost, but not quite, like a human.

The theory behind the uncanny valley effect is that as machines become more human-like, our expectations and evaluations of them change. For example, when they are very different from humans, they are seen as cute or charming, but as they become more human-like, they can cross a threshold into the "uncanny valley," where they are seen as creepy or unsettling.

The uncanny valley effect has important implications for developing robots and artificial intelligence. It suggests that there may be limits to how human-like machines can become before they become off-putting to people. To avoid the uncanny valley, designers and engineers may need to adopt alternative approaches that do not rely on creating highly human-like machines.

Augmenting human talent would be necessary to meet the future's skill demand. Traditional workforces need to be reskilled, upskilled, and powered by AI. Augmenting human talent with AI is highly necessary for the utility industry to support not only the increasing workload but also to gain business efficiency safety and the climate resiliency in the future.

AI replacing humans in the workplace is a complex and highly debated topic that raises important social, economic, and ethical questions. As AI advances, it will be important for policymakers, business leaders, and the public to engage in an informed and nuanced discussion about the potential benefits and risks of AI and how it can be used to create a more equitable and sustainable future.

It's worth noting that the CEO of Facebook, Mark Zuckerberg, has publicly spoken about the role of artificial intelligence (AI) in the future of work and has acknowledged that AI will likely play an increasingly important role in many industries. He has also stated that AI will bring about many benefits, such as increased productivity, improved safety, and new forms of communication. However, he has also acknowledged the potential downsides of AI, such as job displacement and the need for new skills and education to adapt to the changing workforce.

In general, Mark Zuckerberg has a positive view of the role of AI in the future. Still he also recognizes the need for careful consideration of the implications of AI and the need to address the potential downsides responsibly and thoughtfully.

Like those chess-beating computers designed to be smart, they didn't just learn it. Instead, chess-beating computers rely on artificial intelligence techniques, like machine learning, to make these decisions. However, learning is not based on experience or observation in the same way as human learning. Instead, the algorithms are trained on large data sets, and the computer's performance is optimized through trial and error.

So, while chess-beating computers can play chess at a very high level, they have different types of learning and understanding than humans. They are simply following a set of rules and instructions rather than developing an intuition or understanding of the game in the same way a human player might.

The mission will enable the staff members and continue to provide them with more complex tasks, enabling them to produce the most intelligent tools and software. The production would increase tenfold as a result. This will enable businesses to obtain a significant competitive advantage over their rivals. Because they know they won't have to complete any tedious duties today, employees will be much more motivated to show up at work. On the other hand, a word machine can perform a lot of their tedious daily tasks. Future employees will be tested and motivated by their workplace environments, which will help them develop their skill sets and creative ideas. There will be a flourishing of invention, which will be regularly given. Continuous innovation will aid the organization in moving toward the industrial age of new food generation.

Utilities should be able to give the fourth industrial revolution a safe, solid base. Their personnel are the heart and soul of this endeavor and unquestionably the brains behind the organization. AI and machine learning would be potent tools for utility porting.

The ability to alter a business is something that utility companies can offer to their employees. For utilities, having a large talent pool and the ability to maintain that talent pool is crucial. Otherwise, you won't be able to keep your business running. The missing middle would play a role when we combine it all, make a gap between them, and bring them together.

A new set of employment will be produced due to the coexistence of machines and people. For instance, future greet system operators will be equipped with smart tools and resources. They will be better able to anticipate changes and navigate to the actual scenario with its assistance. It will aid in their comprehension of the difficulties facing the Greeks, and based on those recommendations, they will be better prepared to respond. Future field service personnel could remotely inspect while navigating directly to their location. Workers in the utility industry would make up the full front of this intelligently propelled industrial regulation.

Platform Capability

The platform is the foundation of any business. Utilities started their platform journey in the 1990s when they built their mainframe systems to centrally manage their billing metering and customer service functions. The underlying framework for utilities has changed throughout time. They are considering expanding their platform's potential to serve the upcoming energy transition era while converting existing capabilities into cutting-edge cloud-powered applications. One of the main forces behind future success is the transformation of the platforms. Utilities are attempting to accelerate digital transformation projects to create future-proof platform capabilities. These platforms should be intelligently driven by analytics and the Power BI cloud.

New Energy Platform

Our planet is going through a tremendous climate challenge. Energy is one of the biggest contributors to greenhouse gas emissions. Leaders around the world are considering changing the entire energy ecosystem. Significant platform capability investment is needed to transition away from traditional fossil fuels. New resources will be used to fuel new energy. Battery storage would be a significant part of the new energy economy. Integrating traditional conventional and new energy sources and achieving our sustainability goal will require deeper planning and understanding of the overall energy ecosystem. Historical energy platforms would not be sufficient to support this transition or future energy demands. Utility companies must create a platform that can integrate various energy sources, manage customer expectations, and help the world become greener.

Consumers and business people alike are becoming more energizing than ever. Everybody wants to play their part in this sustainability journey. By adding microgrids or other energy storage technologies at the end of the energy pollution, traditional consumers are transitioning to prosumers. This requires a new way of managing energy distribution and transmission. Understanding the overall impact of planning for the future and serving the current needs is the most important thing the new energy platform needs to focus on. Transitioning from a smart guide to a truly digital grid will be done with the help of this new energy platform. Flexibility, transparency, and resiliency would be the key focus ideas for the new energy platform. In addition to assisting corporations on their path, a scalable platform would also assist in making our world greener, satisfying consumer wants, and building viable businesses for the future.

Innovation Platform

A rising number of successful energy innovation platforms and utility firms have discovered new methods for identifying opportunities to deliver economic and societal value. Igniting innovation is an important step in gathering and exposing ideas and concepts from the workforce. Utilities are looking to transition from traditional systems of record to platforms for innovation. Innovation needs to be inclusive, forward-looking, and value-driven. Often, the speed of business change is higher than the system can handle. Innovation platforms must bring the necessary speed to help utilities compete in the new era. The platform should also support optimizing workloads, automating mundane tasks, and providing insights we have never seen before. Testing new ideas, processes, and solutions is the need of the hour. Opening new business opportunities, leveraging new models, and embracing agility are the main outcomes of a universal platform. These innovations conceived by utilities can create new platforms and business models. The new platform will open new revenue streams, which the innovation platform will enable.

Platform Economy

The platform economy is a term that describes the economic and social activities that are enabled by online platforms, which often serve as frameworks for technology or e-commerce. The most common platform type is the "transaction platform," also known as "digital matchmakers," which connects buyers and sellers. Examples of transaction platforms include Amazon, Airbnb, Uber, and Baidu.

To become a platform player, utilities must invest in four critical technological dimensions: cloud, data, AI, and APIs. By leveraging the power of these technologies, utilities can create a service platform that connects partners and customers with the help of cloud-based solutions. Access to a rich data set can be monetized through the platform economy API, empowering utilities to connect with the larger ecosystem. Additionally, the Yayan intelligence award decision-making system can be used by utilities to identify new revenue streams and make better decisions. Utilities can use their large data sets to support other businesses in understanding the needs and preferences of their clients by providing building services for future homes and satellite services.

Additionally, utilities can generate new revenue streams by developing and offering new YAI capabilities as services. One example of such a service is image analytics which uses machine learning in grid infrastructure which many utilities invest in for fault detection and asset health analytics. San Diego Gas and Electric have already developed such a use case. The EPI (platform economy API) will help utilities monetize their platform capabilities by exposing them to other businesses.

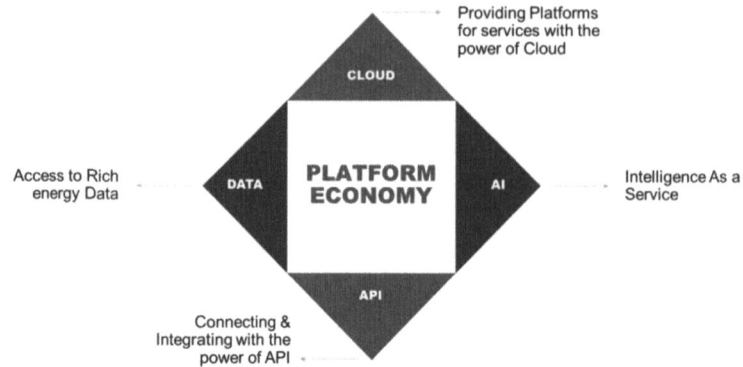

Key Takeaways

- Key takeaways for utilities to benefit from the potential offered by the digital age, they must concentrate on becoming digital energy companies. As a result, they must concentrate on offering their clients digital energy services like demand response and energy efficiency initiatives.

- In addition, utilities must focus on developing new digital technologies to help them better manage the electric grid and provide more reliable and affordable electricity to their customers.

- A total transformation of utilities focused on technology, people, and business model is needed to address many of the challenges faced by utilities, our environment, and society.

- Utilizing cloud, data, AI, and API is transforming the energy sector and helping utilities to better serve their customers.

- Utilities can improve operations, provide better services, and create new business opportunities by leveraging these technologies.

CHAPTER 4

AI Adoption in Utilities

AI is rapidly changing the overall technology and business world by introducing essential automation tools to game-changing solutions like driverless cars, Amazon Go, etc. Tech companies are pioneers in adopting AI. However, non-tech companies are also racing for AI adoption. Due to a lack of knowledge on the adoption status of AI and where their competitors are going, companies can experience the wait-or-adopt syndrome. Also, companies planning or recently starting their AI journey without an effective AI adoption strategy face significant roadblocks.

Artificial intelligence (AI) is one of our most important emerging technologies, with the potential to transform nearly every industry. AI is already being leveraged in the utility sector to control the electrical grid, optimize energy use, and foresee equipment faults. Utilities are anticipated to utilize it increasingly as technology develops to stay competitive and provide consumers with the best service possible.

The global AI market in the utility sector was valued at $1.4 billion in 2018 and is projected to reach $10.8 billion by 2025, growing at a compound annual growth rate (CAGR) of 38.1%, according to a report by MarketsandMarkets. Several factors, including the increasing need for energy efficiency, the rapid growth of renewable energy sources, and the aging of the existing electricity grid, drive this growth. Nevertheless, there are still a lot of obstacles to be solved before AI can truly take off in the utility sector. One of the biggest challenges is data. Utilities generate much

D. Roy, *AI for Utilities*, https://doi.org/10.1007/979-8-8688-0202-7_4

data, but it is often siloed and not easily accessible. Another challenge is the lack of standardization. There are many different types of utilities, each with unique challenges and requirements.

In the past, utilities largely relied on traditional methods of managing the grid, such as manually controlling switches and breakers. However, given the complexity of the infrastructure, increased demand for electricity, and supply variability, this is no longer practical. Instead, AI provides a way for utilities to automatically control the grid, using algorithms to make real-time decisions about how to best meet demand.

AI's capacity to assist in managing the growing amount of renewable energy on the grid is one of the most important advantages it offers to utilities. The power system must adapt as renewable energy sources like wind and solar grow more prevalent to handle supply fluctuation. AI can be used to predict when renewable energy sources will be available and dispatch them to meet demand.

In addition, AI can be used to optimize energy usage by predicting when demand will be high and implementing measures to reduce consumption. For example, AI can control air conditioning and lighting in office buildings during periods of low occupancy, thereby reducing overall energy consumption and lowering costs for end users. While this may not directly lower the price of energy, it does reduce demand during peak times, which can help prevent price spikes and enhance the overall efficiency of the grid.

AI is also being used to predict equipment failures by analyzing sensor data to identify patterns that indicate an impending failure. This allows utilities to take preventive action to avoid outages and improve the grid's reliability.

The utility sector is just beginning to scratch the surface of what AI can do. To stay competitive and provide their customers with the best service possible, utilities will likely employ AI in greater numbers as technology advances.

Factors Influencing the Adoption

In the past few years, there has been a lot of hype around artificial intelligence (AI) and its potential to revolutionize various industries. The utility industry is no exception. In fact, AI is already starting to have a significant impact on the utility sector, with several companies investing in this technology.

The adoption of AI in the utility industry is influenced by a variety of factors, including

1. **Cost**: Implementing and maintaining AI systems hinder adoption for some utilities, especially smaller companies with limited resources.

2. **Regulation**: The regulatory environment plays a significant role in the adoption of AI in the utility industry. Regulations that support innovation and the use of new technologies can facilitate the adoption of AI. However, the regulatory framework also impacts how investments in AI are classified and paid for, particularly in terms of capital versus operating expenses. For instance, utility companies may face challenges in justifying AI investments if they are treated as operating expenses, which are subject to tighter budget constraints compared to capital expenditures. Clear regulatory guidance on how AI-related costs can be recovered through rate structures is crucial for encouraging sustained investment and integration of AI technologies into utility operations.

3. **Technical expertise**: The availability of technical expertise and skilled personnel is crucial in adopting AI. Utilities need access to individuals with expertise in data analysis, machine learning, and AI development to effectively implement these technologies.

4. **Data quality and availability**: Data quality and availability are key factors in the success of AI initiatives. High-quality data is needed to train AI models and make accurate predictions, and utilities must have systems to collect and manage this data.

5. **Organizational culture**: The willingness of a utility to embrace new technologies and innovative approaches can play a role in the adoption of AI. Utilities open to new ideas and willing to take risks are more likely to adopt AI and other new technologies.

6. **Economic benefits**: The potential economic benefits of AI, such as improved efficiency, reduced costs, and increased revenue, can be a significant driver of adoption in the utility industry.

7. **Competition**: Competition from other utilities and new entrants to the market can also influence the adoption of AI. Utilities that want to stay ahead may adopt AI to gain a competitive advantage.

Overall, the adoption of AI in the utility industry is influenced by a combination of technical, economic, regulatory, and organizational factors. By understanding these factors, utilities can make informed decisions about adopting AI and realize its full potential.

AI can help utilities to become more efficient and to reduce operating costs. AI can also help utilities to improve customer service and to better manage assets.

Utility providers can use AI to estimate water/heating/energy consumption and thus come up with dynamic pricing to give super inexpensive options when there is excess capacity, for example.

Through advanced disaggregation and consumer segmentation, AI delivers a highly individualized perspective of household interactions with various products. Advanced disaggregation refers to the process of breaking down overall energy usage into specific components, such as identifying the energy consumption of individual appliances within a household. This allows customers to see a detailed view of their energy use, helping them to understand which devices or habits contribute most to their bills. As a result, customers concerned about bill size can make informed decisions to alter and limit their utility consumption in the most effective way.

The lack of knowledge about AI in the utility sector is one of the significant obstacles to its adoption. Many utilities still need to be made aware of the potential of AI and how it can be used to improve their operations. In addition, there needs to be more skilled AI personnel in the utility sector. This is a major challenge since utilities need access to skilled AI personnel to develop and implement AI-based solutions.

Another challenge that utilities face is the lack of data. Many utilities need access to the necessary data to train AI algorithms. This is a major barrier since data is essential for AI applications.

Despite the challenges, there are several reasons why utilities should consider investing in AI. AI can assist utilities in increasing efficiency, enhancing customer service, and better managing their assets. In addition, AI can help utilities to better cope with the challenges posed by the increasing penetration of renewable energy sources.

Organizational Factors

Organizational factors significantly influence the adoption of artificial intelligence (AI) in the utility industry. Some of the key organizational factors are mentioned below.

1. **Organizational culture:** A company that is open to new ideas and technologies is more likely to adopt AI than a company that is resistant to change.

2. **Organizational structure:** A company's structure can influence its approach to adopting AI, though the impact can vary depending on other factors like leadership and organizational culture. A centralized, hierarchical company might have the advantage of implementing AI at scale more quickly if leadership is strongly committed to the initiative. In contrast, a decentralized, flat organization might foster innovation and experimentation with AI, allowing different departments to explore and adopt AI tools that best meet their specific needs. However, this decentralized approach could also lead to fragmented efforts with less cohesive impact. Ultimately, the success of AI adoption depends on how well the company aligns its structure with strategic goals and supports AI integration across the organization.

3. **Organizational size:** The size of a company can influence its approach to adopting AI, though the relationship is not straightforward. Larger companies often have more resources, including capital, talent, and infrastructure, which can make it easier for them to invest in AI technologies and

scale their implementation. They may also have more complex operations that can benefit from AI-driven efficiencies. However, small companies might be more agile, allowing them to experiment with and adopt AI quickly without the bureaucratic hurdles that can slow down larger organizations. The decision to adopt AI is often influenced more by a company's strategic priorities, leadership commitment, and market pressures than by size alone.

4. **Organizational resources:** The resources of a company also play a role in influencing its willingness to adopt AI. A company having the financial resources and the human resources required to implement AI is more likely to adopt AI than a company that does not have these resources.

5. **Organizational goals:** The goals of a company significantly influence its decision to adopt AI. While most companies aim for some form of competitive advantage, the specific context matters. For instance, in the utility sector, where companies often operate as quasi-monopolists, the focus may be less on outpacing competitors and more on providing high-quality, low-cost service. In such cases, AI adoption is driven by goals like reducing operational costs, improving service reliability, and enhancing customer satisfaction, rather than simply gaining a competitive edge. A company with a strong commitment to efficiency, cost reduction, and service improvement is more likely to invest in AI as a strategic tool to achieve these objectives.

69

Environmental Factor

The 21st century has seen a dramatic increase in technological advances, with one of the most significant being the rise of artificial intelligence (AI). AI has the potential to revolutionize the utility industry, providing significant improvements in efficiency and productivity. However, adopting AI in the utility industry could be faster due partly to the sector's complex and regulated nature. Many environmental factors have influenced the adoption of AI in the utility industry. One of the most significant is the cost of AI technology. AI technology is still in its infancy and is expensive to develop and deploy. Adoption has been severely hampered by this, especially for smaller utility companies.

The regulatory environment is also a significant factor influencing the adoption of AI in the utility sector. The sector is highly regulated, and utility companies are required to comply with a range of regulations, including those relating to safety, security, and privacy. This compliance burden can be a major deterrent to adopting new technologies, such as AI.

Despite the challenges, there are various reasons why the utility sector is well suited to adopting AI. Utility firms are already gathering a lot of data on their consumers and operations in this data-rich industry. This data can be used to train AI applications and to improve their accuracy and performance.

Technological Factors

The low cost and high availability of computing power is the primary factor driving the adoption of AI. In addition, the development of new and more powerful AI algorithms, and the increasing availability of data sets that can be used to train AI models, are also playing a role in adopting AI technology.

The difficulty of collecting data and management is one of the main technological factors influencing the adoption of AI in the utility industry. AI technology is only as good as the data it is based on, and utility companies often have large and complex data sets that can be difficult to collect and manage. Another challenge is integrating AI technology into existing systems and processes. Utility companies often have legacy systems designed to work with new technologies, making adopting AI-based solutions difficult.

AI Adoption Maturity Model for Utilities

Utility companies are looking at AI and ML to improve efficiency and optimize operations. But these technologies can be complex and challenging to implement. So, where should you start, and how do you move forward?

Using the AI Adoption Maturity Model, which I have developed specifically for utilities, organizations can progress through a series of growth phases and effectively manage crisis points. This model provides a structured framework for utilities to assess their current level of AI integration, identify areas for improvement, and strategically plan for future advancements, ensuring a robust and adaptive approach to AI adoption.

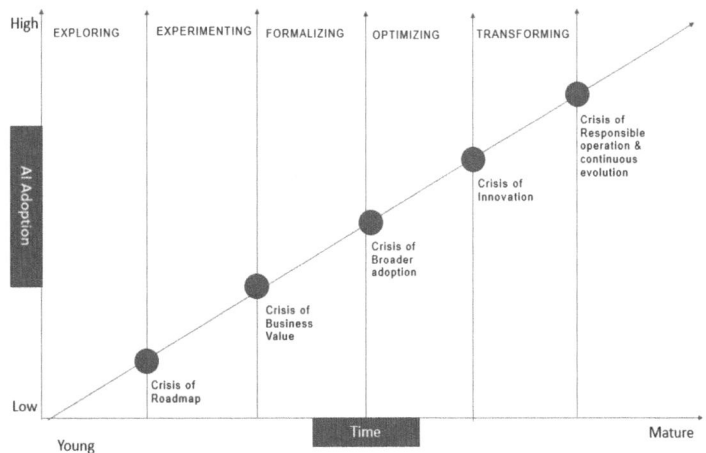

Exploring

During the exploring phase, utilities learn about various AI solutions available in the market and their feasibility in solving their problems. If the AI solution is feasible, they will go for the pilot phase to test it on their data. But unfortunately, the exploration phase can often go in a different direction and end up with a roadmap crisis.

Experimenting

To evolve from the crisis of roadmap, organizations try to narrow down the focus area for experimenting with AI solutions at a smaller scale. Different solutions are conceptualized and utilized in the business context through these experiments. End of this phase, organizations try to understand the business value they can get from the AI investment.

Formalizing

Organizations start formalizing AI adoption in the enterprise context to establish the business value framework in the next stage. It starts getting embedded into the values of product lines and business functions. Problems are solved using AI solutions, various use cases emerge, and businesses start seeing value. Often it focuses on standard AI use cases, model development, and automation. This phase ends with the crisis of broader adoption, where the organization starts thinking about the art of possibilities, newer ideas, and scaling the AI.

Optimizing

Once AI solutions start scaling, the need for optimized use of resources comes into play. So, how do we cut down noises, eliminate unproductive use cases, and start focusing on fundamental business transformation?

This phase ends with the crisis of innovation, where the organization starts thinking about reinventing its business models and doing true innovation using AI and opening new revenue streams.

Transforming

Transforming is the final phase where total Enterprise reinvention happens. AI gets considered as a value driver, not only an automation tool. It becomes a creative part of the business strategy. Strategic discussions happen around an AI-based roadmap. This phase starts the responsible operation crisis and AI solutions' continuous evolution.

Key Takeaways

- Utilities are laggards in AI adoption, and many utilities don't even know how to start. But the ones that have are seeing a lot of benefits.

- The increasing need for improved customer service, the desire to be more proactive, and the expectation of more personalized service are all drivers for the utility industry to adopt AI.

- However, several challenges need to be considered when adopting AI, including data privacy and security concerns, the need for skilled workers, and the potential for disruptions to the power grid.

- As AI and Machine Learning technologies continue to evolve, utilities are expected to increasingly turn to these technologies to help them improve their operations and better meet the needs of their customers.

CHAPTER 5

Sustainability Imperative for Utilities

In this chapter, we will explore the sustainability imperative for utilities and its implications for the industry's future. We will examine the challenges utilities face in meeting customers' sustainability needs and how these challenges can be addressed. We will also discuss technology's role in helping utilities meet sustainability goals and the increasing importance of sustainability-focused investments in the utility sector. Finally, we will look at the implications of the sustainability imperative for utilities and the opportunities it presents for the industry.

Introduction

As the world moves toward a cleaner energy future, the importance of sustainability in the utility sector will only grow. In the United States, coal-fired power plants account for 42% of carbon emissions, according to data from the US Environmental Protection Agency (EPA).

Additionally, utilities will be compelled to use imported coal or natural gas as their primary fuel sources as the United States' supply of low-sulfur coal runs out. This transition will come with high environmental costs as these energy sources produce significantly more carbon emissions.

Climate change is predicted to worsen the situation by increasing storm frequency and intensity. These storms can wreak havoc on power

D. Roy, *AI for Utilities*, https://doi.org/10.1007/979-8-8688-0202-7_5

grids, causing blackouts and extensive damage to power plants. As the United States moves away from coal and increasingly relies on natural gas and solar power, there is a risk of energy dependence if the transition leads to over-reliance on a single alternative fuel source. Diversifying energy sources is crucial to reduce the risk associated with dependence on any one source, whether it be coal, natural gas, or solar power. The goal is to create a balanced energy portfolio that can ensure stability and resilience in the energy supply. Sustainable operations are essential for all businesses today, but are particularly critical for utilities as they serve imperative social functions. Utilities must operate their power plants and delivery systems reliably and efficiently, providing affordable and reliable power to their customers. They must also be mindful of their environmental impact, comply with regulations, and invest in technologies to minimize the adverse effects of their activities.

Additionally, they must be aware of the social consequences of their actions and work with their stakeholders to meet the needs and worries of their clients, staff members, and the communities in which they operate. In this chapter, I'll discuss key utility drivers, such as an ability journey. I will also share some of the case studies related to AI and sustainability, which are highly relevant to the utility industry.

Governmental Regulation

In recent years, there has been an increased focus on sustainability from governments around the world. This has led to several regulations being put in place to drive sustainability initiatives.

One of the most notable examples is the Paris Agreement, ratified by over 190 countries in 2016. The agreement sets many goals for reducing greenhouse gas emissions to combat climate change.

In the United States, the Clean Power Plan was introduced by the Obama administration in 2015. The plan aims to reduce carbon dioxide emissions from power plants by 32% by 2030.

Many other countries have also introduced similar regulations. For example, in the European Union, the Renewable Energy Directive requires that 20% of all energy come from renewable sources by 2020. China has also set a target of 20% renewable energy by 2030.

These regulations have a positive impact on the development of sustainable technologies. For example, the solar industry's growth has been driven partly by government incentives. The increase in sustainability regulations is a positive step toward combating climate change and protecting the environment. However, these regulations must be properly enforced to ensure they are effective.

Carbon Pollution-Free Electricity Policy

The emission of carbon dioxide from power stations would be prohibited under a carbon pollution-free electricity policy. The policy would also aim to increase the use of renewable energy sources, such as solar and wind power, and to reduce the use of fossil fuels, such as coal and natural gas.

There are numerous advantages to an electrical policy devoid of carbon pollution. It would reduce the amount of carbon dioxide in the atmosphere, a greenhouse gas contributing to climate change. The initiative would also lessen dependency on fossil fuels, a limited resource, and generate jobs in the renewable energy industry. However, the implementation of a carbon pollution-free electricity policy has its challenges. The expense of switching to renewable energy sources is the major obstacle. While solar and wind power have historically been more expensive than fossil fuels, their costs have been decreasing and are nearing comparability in certain circumstances. However, the issue isn't just about price – it's also about the variability of solar and wind power, which can lead to instability in the electricity grid without appropriate energy storage solutions. Additionally, the effectiveness and cost-efficiency of solar and wind power can be influenced by geographic factors, such as proximity to ideal locations for these energy sources. As a result, policies promoting renewable energy may still lead to higher electricity prices in some regions, depending on these factors.

Several variables, such as the project's size and location, the technology employed, and complexity, can considerably impact the cost of establishing wind- and solar-generating facilities.

According to the US Department of Energy, the average cost of installing a utility-scale solar power plant in the United States was $1.75 per watt in 2020, ranging from $1.50 per watt for large projects to $2.00 per watt for smaller projects. These costs can vary depending on the project's location, with costs generally being lower in sunny states like California and Arizona.

The cost of installing a wind power plant can vary depending on the size and location of the project. According to the US Department of Energy, the average cost of installing a utility-scale wind power plant in the United States was $1.80 per watt in 2020, ranging from $1.60 per watt for large projects to $2.20 per watt for smaller projects. These costs may also differ based on the project's location, with costs often lower in regions with abundant wind resources.

For comparison, the cost of installing a natural gas power plant generally ranges from $0.90 to $1.20 per watt, making it less expensive than wind in terms of upfront installation costs. Coal power plants, although less commonly built today due to environmental concerns, typically have installation costs ranging from $2.00 to $3.00 per watt. However, these costs do not account for the long-term operational and environmental costs associated with fossil fuels, which can make renewables like wind more competitive over time.

It's important to note that these costs are only estimates and can vary significantly depending on the project. The entire cost of establishing a wind or solar power plant might vary depending on the project's complexity, the type of technology employed, and the location of the facility.

There is also the challenge of storage for renewable energy. Solar and wind power are intermittent, so they must be stored to provide power when the sun is not shining, or the wind is not blowing.

A carbon pollution-free power strategy is essential to halting climate change and safeguarding the environment, notwithstanding the difficulties. The benefits of the policy far outweigh the costs, and the transition to renewable energy is an investment in the future.

CarbonSim: EDF's carbon market simulation tool

The European Union (EU) has established a carbon market to meet its ambitious climate goals. This market allows companies to trade carbon emissions permits, incentivizing the reduction of greenhouse gas emissions. The Environmental Defense Fund (EDF) has created CarbonSim, a tool that simulates the EU carbon market. CarbonSim allows users to create a virtual power plant and trade carbon permits on a simulated market. The product is designed to help businesses understand how the carbon market functions and how they can effectively utilize it to reduce their emissions. CarbonSim is a valuable tool for companies looking to reduce their emissions in alignment with the EU's climate goals, enabling them to make informed decisions about trading carbon permits.

The tool can help companies to understand the carbon market and to make informed decisions about how to trade carbon permits. CarbonSim is a valuable tool for companies looking to reduce their emissions to meet the EU's climate goals.

Zero-Emission Vehicle Policy

An electric vehicle (EV) or a plug-in hybrid is not necessarily a zero-emission vehicle based on what type of energy source is used to generate the electricity used to charge it. Combining fossil fuels and renewable energy sources must generate the electricity that powers EVs. Therefore, consideration must be given to the environmental impact of electricity production in choosing the most appropriate vehicle for an individual's daily driving needs.

To promote the adoption of electric vehicles, many governments offer tax breaks or other incentives to consumers who purchase EVs, impose stricter emissions standards for new cars, or create a public charging infrastructure. Some government entities also provide rebates or other incentives to businesses that purchase EVs or install charging stations.

These regulations emphasize promoting natural gas, electric, and other low-emission automobiles. Governments can implement these policies by providing rebates and other financial incentives to encourage people to buy greener cars, enhancing public transportation, or tightening emissions regulations for currently registered vehicles.

Enel X and global AI software platform OptiBus: A partnership that's committed to zero-emission fleets

Enel X, a global leader in advanced energy services, and Optibus, an AI software platform for intelligent transportation, announced a strategic partnership to help public and private fleet operators around the world transition to zero-emission vehicles.

The partnership will see Enel X provide its expertise in electric vehicle (EV) charging infrastructure and energy management to Optibus, which will use its AI technology to optimize fleet operations and maximize the benefits of electrification.

The partnership aims to accelerate the global transition to zero-emission fleets, essential for tackling climate change and air pollution. Although electric vehicles are already more cost-effective and environmentally friendly than petrol or diesel, their adoption has been hindered by a dearth of charging stations and worries over range anxiety.

Range anxiety is what an electric vehicle (EV) driver feels when the battery charge is low, and the usual sources of electricity are unavailable.

It sparks a fear of getting stranded somewhere, which adds time, inconvenience, and stress to a journey. Studies show that driving range, cost, and a lack of charging infrastructure are why people do not consider EVs when buying a new vehicle.

Enel X and Optibus will work together to address these challenges and make electric fleets the norm rather than the exception. Enel X will provide extensive experience in designing and operating EV charging infrastructure. At the same time, Optibus will use its AI platform to optimize fleet operations and ensure that electric vehicles are used as efficiently as possible.

The partnership will also see Enel X and Optibus collaborate on research and development projects to accelerate the transition to electric fleets. This will include working on new technologies and applications that can further improve the efficiency of electric fleets.

The partnership between Enel X and Optibus is an example of the types of collaborations that are crucial in transitioning to a low-carbon future and creating a cleaner, healthier planet. While this specific partnership is important, it highlights the need for many more similar initiatives across various sectors to effectively combat climate change and promote sustainability

Net-Zero Building Emissions Policy

Net-Zero Buildings are designed to produce more energy than they consume. Net-Zero Energy Buildings produce as much energy as they consume, but they do not necessarily produce more. Net-Zero Emissions Buildings focus on reducing greenhouse gas emissions to as close to zero as possible. The most sustainable and ideal scenario would be Net-Zero Emissions and Energy Buildings, which aim to achieve both minimal emissions and balanced energy consumption. However, achieving this level of sustainability may not be feasible in every situation. For example, a net-zero emissions building might be in a city with an unreliable power grid and rely on rooftop solar panels and a battery storage system to power the building during outages.

The United States has a long way to go to meet its climate goals, and buildings account for nearly 40% of all energy consumption. EPA regulations on emissions from power plants have made it easier to generate electricity from natural gas, but it is challenging and costs more to upgrade buildings. While building new, carbon-neutral buildings is an important part of addressing the climate challenge, it is equally crucial to focus on retrofitting existing buildings to reduce their carbon emissions. Rather than implying the need to replace all current buildings, the goal should be a combination of constructing new, sustainable buildings and upgrading the energy efficiency and carbon footprint of the existing building stock. This comprehensive approach is more practical and effective in tackling the climate challenge.

To reduce carbon emissions, many countries have adopted policies to promote the use of renewable energy. These policies may be enacted at the national or local level and may apply to all or specific types of buildings. However, owners and managers may find it difficult to comply with laws governing energy efficiency and lowering carbon emissions from buildings, mainly when those structures already exist. A building emissions policy can help in these situations by offering monetary incentives.

With AI, ENGIE is revolutionizing the management of next-gen buildings

ENGIE is using AI to transform the way that next-generation buildings are managed. Using AI to analyze data from smart meters and other sensors, ENGIE can predict energy usage and maintenance requirements more accurately than ever. Engineers can be more proactive about maintenance, reducing the risk of unexpected outages.

The company's AI-powered software can be integrated into any building's control system and used to optimize energy consumption. The AI system of a building can gather data on consumption patterns, climate, and other factors to decide when to turn on the heating or cooling systems. It can also be used to control lighting, ventilation, and other building systems to optimize energy consumption. An AI system can also be used to collect information about the health of the building's equipment to determine when to schedule maintenance.

Real-time data is gathered and analyzed to provide clients a more individualized experience (e.g., adjusting lighting and climate settings based on your schedule or preferences). In addition, these technologies reduce operational costs by optimizing maintenance schedules, identifying problems before they occur, and collecting data from equipment to improve the design of new buildings.

Climate-Resilient Infrastructure and Operations

Infrastructure is critical to the smooth functioning of businesses and societies. Sadly, the infrastructure that keeps our societies running, such as power grids, highways, and water systems, is frequently constructed with little regard for the effects of climate change. As a result, these systems are more likely to break down due to climate-related events, which can have a ripple effect on other critical systems. Investing in climate-resilient infrastructure and operations can help prevent these breakdowns, and maintain critical systems when needed, and reduce the risk of climate-related disruptions to businesses and societies.

The shift to a low-carbon economy will require significant investment in infrastructure, with some estimates as high as $75 trillion by 2050. New infrastructure must be climate resilient to make the most of this investment and continue to be robust to climate change. Climate-resilient infrastructure is designed to withstand extreme weather, maintain functionality during and after extreme weather events, and be upgradeable to accommodate future climate changes.

In the context of climate change, resilient infrastructure and operations can withstand the impacts of climate change and continue to meet their intended purpose. An infrastructure or operation is considered climate-resilient in the context of resilience when it can endure climatic change and still serve its original purpose. Climate-resilient infrastructure and operations are particularly critical for communities dependent on a single industry or natural resource for their economic well-being.

National Grid Reduces Damages by 22% in 1 Year

National Grid lowered its damage rate (the number of damages per 1000 811 tickets) in the jurisdiction of downstate New York by applying universal subsurface damage avoidance best practices. For context, "811 tickets" refer to requests made by contractors or homeowners before digging to ensure underground utilities are marked and avoided. As a result of these best practices, the utility's damage rate decreased by 65 percent, from 5.36 damages per thousand in 2006 to 1.89 damages per thousand in 2014. However, after several years of improvement, the utility's damage rate reached a plateau.

National Grid collaborated with Urbint to build Lens for Damage Prevention, an artificial intelligence-powered program that detects high-risk excavations. To assign risk scores to 811 tickets, Urbint Lens examines a utility's historical incident data and internal data such as asset age, type, and location, and combines it with Urbint's Model of the World – a representation of external forces surrounding and impacting underground assets such as soil conditions, elevation, weather, population density, and construction.

Consumer and Shareholder Demands

A decrease in coal-fired power plants and an increase in investment in renewable energy sources like solar and wind are projected to follow the transition to cleaner energy sources and a more sustainable energy mix. The transition to clean energy requires increasing investments in energy efficiency technologies. In addition, traditional consumers and shareholders are becoming more aware of sustainable business practices. They are demanding to invest in more businesses that practice sustainability.

Sustainability-Themed Investment

The environment may be protected while you make money by investing in environmentally friendly businesses. Sustainable investment can be done in a variety of ways. Some investments are in for-profit companies actively trying to make the world a better place. Other investments in sustainability are in non-profit organizations working to solve social and environmental problems.

There are many ways to invest in sustainability.

Investments in sustainability can come with significant risks, both financial and non-financial. Beyond the potential financial risks, such as uncertain returns or high up-front costs, there are also regulatory, technological, and reputational risks. Regulatory risks arise from changing environmental laws and policies that could impact the viability of certain investments. Technological risks involve the uncertainty of adopting new or unproven technologies that may not perform as expected. Reputational risks occur if sustainability efforts fail or are perceived as "greenwashing," potentially damaging a company's public image. Despite these risks, sustainability investments also have the potential for very high returns, particularly as markets increasingly prioritize environmental responsibility. Researching the companies or organizations you want to invest in can help avoid risk. So, how to invest in sustainability? You can choose a broker or other financial advisor, or you can choose to buy stocks or mutual funds.

It is important that the money you save is used to create a financial future. So, why not use the savings to create a more sustainable future? Putting money into green, clean, and other sustainability-related industries can increase your portfolio while simultaneously helping the environment. Over the past few years, many companies with a sustainability focus have increased stock value, creating a fantastic investment opportunity. Investors looking to put their money into a company promoting green initiatives can look for stocks involved in clean energy generation, research, and development of sustainable products, recycling or waste management, or eco-friendly manufacturing. These stocks may have a higher risk than traditional investments but can offer higher returns.

Clarity AI provides ESG-related asset allocation customization capabilities

In recent years, many institutional investors have shown an increased interest in environmental, social, and governance (ESG) factors when making investment decisions. However, a lack of data and transparency around ESG issues has made it difficult for investors to integrate these factors into their investment processes.

Clarity AI is a financial technology company that provides ESG-related asset allocation customization capabilities for institutional investors. The company's platform uses artificial intelligence (AI) to analyze a range of data sources, including company filings, news articles, and social media posts, to generate customized ESG portfolios for investors.

Clarity AI's platform offers various advantages for investors interested in integrating ESG factors into asset allocation decisions. First, the platform offers great flexibility, enabling investors to adjust their portfolios by their unique preferences regarding ESG. Second, the platform is constantly updated with the latest data and information, giving investors a real-time view of companies' performance on ESG issues. Third, the platform's AI-based methodology also enables it to recognize and analyze a variety of data sources, giving investors a thorough understanding of a company's ESG performance. As a result, the Clarity AI platform provides a valuable tool for investors interested in incorporating ESG factors into their asset allocation decisions. Finally, the platform's ability to customize portfolios and its real-time data and information allows investors to make well-informed investment decisions that align with their ESG preferences.

ESG Activism by Investors

ESG investing is driven by the desire to make money while doing good. In researching stocks or other investments, investors can discover that some companies they are considering investing in have objectionable or unsustainable practices. To voice their concerns, these investors can then get in touch with the business and the organization offering the investment. The firm can then respond by dropping the investment from its offerings or engaging with the company to discuss its policies and how they might be changed to eliminate the investors' concerns. ESG investing is a growing trend among investors, and many fund providers cater to the demand. However, most mutual funds are still non-ESG compliant.

Investors who want to invest in socially conscious funds have a few options. You can invest in a diversified fund that meets some ESG criteria or pick a fund dedicated to a particular cause. The latter choice might be wiser for your financial objectives, but you'll probably have to take on greater risk. The good news is that most large fund providers offer at least one ESG-friendly fund. Vanguard, BlackRock, and State Street all offer ESG-friendly funds. These companies have ESG criteria when considering which companies to invest in.

ESG (Environmental, Social, and Governance) investing has gained recognition as a profitable long-term strategy, with numerous studies and reports supporting its financial benefits. For example, several analyses have shown that companies with strong ESG practices often demonstrate better risk management and resilience, leading to more stable and sustainable returns over time. However, beyond financial performance, investors are increasingly considering the social and environmental impacts of the companies they invest in, aligning their investments with their values and broader societal goals. This awareness has led to the rise of socially responsible investing or SRI.

SRI is choosing stocks based on a company's social and environmental policies, impact, and financial performance. Many investors are also interested in sustainability, which is the ability of a company's business model to meet the needs of current and future generations without compromising the ability of future generations to meet their own needs.

Investing in socially responsible or sustainable companies can potentially lead to greater profits and a risk reduction. However, it's no secret that today's business climate is volatile. Numerous factors, ranging from the fluctuating price of oil to the unpredictability of emerging markets, might have a detrimental impact on the financial health of your retirement account.

ESG Measurement and Reporting

An ESG report is a financial statement that includes non-financial data that investors may consider an additional risk factor. This can be a standardized ESG report or a non-standardized report that includes a company's unique ESG considerations. The standardized report includes company-specific information, such as its industry, location, and size. A standardized ESG report is like an SRI report, but an SRI report does not include non-financial information. An ESG report is similar to a non-IFRS financial report, but it focuses on non-financial information. For context, IFRS stands for International Financial Reporting Standards, which are a set of accounting standards developed by the International Accounting Standards Board (IASB) to provide a global framework for how public companies prepare and disclose their financial statements. While IFRS reports cover financial performance, ESG reports provide insights into a company's environmental, social, and governance practices, offering a broader perspective on its overall impact and sustainability.

Decreasing Cost of Renewable Energy

Renewable energy costs have been decreasing rapidly and, in many cases, are now becoming cost-competitive with fossil fuels. However, the cost comparison can vary depending on specific circumstances, such as location, scale, and the availability of storage solutions. While renewables are increasingly affordable, certain factors, such as variability and geographic considerations, can still influence overall costs compared to fossil fuels. Solar panels and wind turbines have dropped in cost by more than 70% since the mid-2000s, making them an increasingly cost-effective way to generate electricity. Governments are also attempting to level the playing field by boosting subsidies for renewable energy development while decreasing contributions to produce fossil fuels. Renewable energy costs have decreased significantly in recent years due to technological advances, increased investment, and economies of scale. In many cases, renewable energy costs are comparable to or even cheaper than traditional energy sources. This has made renewable energy a more attractive option for utilities, businesses, and individuals looking to reduce their carbon footprint and move toward a more sustainable energy future.

Decrease in the Cost of Geothermal Energy

Geothermal energy is energy generated from the heat of the Earth's core. It can be harnessed to produce electricity or for heating and cooling applications. Geothermal energy is considered renewable because it is replenished by the Earth's internal heat source. The decreasing cost of geothermal energy can be attributed to several factors, including:

1. Improved technology and drilling methods

2. Increased investment and funding

3. Expansion of geothermal plants and increased efficiency

4. Government incentives and tax credits

5. More competition in the market

6. Increased public awareness and demand

Decrease in the Cost of Hydropower

Hydropower is energy generated from water movement, typically from a dam or water turbine. Hydropower is considered renewable because water is replenished through precipitation and runoff. The decreasing cost of hydropower can be attributed to several factors, including:

1. Improved technology and automation

2. Increased investment and funding

3. Expansion of hydropower plants and increased efficiency

4. Government incentives and tax credits

5. More competition in the market

6. Improved project planning and execution

7. Reduced financing costs

Fall in the Cost of Ocean Energy

Ocean energy refers to energy derived from the ocean, including tidal, wave, and thermal energy. Ocean energy is considered renewable because the ocean is replenished by the sun and wind. The decreasing cost of ocean energy can be attributed to several factors, including:

1. Improved technology and innovation

2. Increased investment and funding

3. Expansion of ocean energy projects

4. Government incentives and tax credits

5. More competition in the market

6. Improved engineering and design

7. Advancements in materials science

Dip in the Cost of Bioenergy

Bioenergy is energy generated from organic matter, such as crops, wood, and waste. It is considered renewable because organic matter can be replenished through sustainable agriculture and forestry practices. The decreasing cost of bioenergy can be attributed to several key factors:

1. **Increased Investment and Funding:** Growing interest from both public and private sectors has led to more capital being funneled into bioenergy research and development, accelerating advancements and scaling production.

2. **Expansion of Bioenergy Projects:** As more bioenergy projects come online, economies of scale are being realized, reducing overall production costs and making bioenergy more competitive with traditional energy sources.

3. **Improved Technology and Automation:** Advances in technology, including more efficient conversion processes and automation in bioenergy production, have significantly lowered operational costs and increased output.

4. **Government Incentives and Tax Credits:** Policies such as subsidies, tax credits, and grants have played a crucial role in lowering the financial barriers to bioenergy adoption, making it more accessible and affordable.

5. **More Competition in the Market:** As more companies enter the bioenergy market, competition drives innovation and cost reduction, leading to more efficient and cost-effective solutions.

6. **Increased Availability of Feedstocks:** Improved agricultural practices and better waste management have led to a more reliable and abundant supply of organic feedstocks, reducing the cost of raw materials needed for bioenergy production.

7. **Improved Conversion Processes:** Research into new methods of converting organic matter into energy, such as advanced bio-refining techniques, has led to more efficient processes that maximize energy output while minimizing waste and costs.

These developments reflect the broader trends in the bioenergy sector, where ongoing research and technological innovation are driving significant improvements, making bioenergy an increasingly viable and cost-effective renewable energy source.

Fallen Solar Power Price

While solar and wind energy costs have historically been higher than those of fossil fuels, they are rapidly decreasing due to technological improvements. In many cases, solar and wind energy are becoming cost-competitive with fossil fuels, especially when considering long-term operational and environmental benefits. However, the cost can still vary depending on specific factors like location, scale, and storage solutions. Solar panel costs have fallen by 50% since 2011, and solar energy is becoming more competitive as an alternative to fossil fuels. Wind energy costs have also fallen, and the US Department of Energy expects them to decline by another 20–30% by 2030. As these costs continue to decrease, we expect to see increased adoption of renewable energy sources.

Scientists harness machine learning to lower solar energy cost

Solar energy is one of the most promising renewable energy sources, but its high cost has been a major barrier to its widespread adoption. A 2021 study by Cornell University shows that machine learning can reduce the cost of solar energy by up to 20%, primarily by optimizing the development of low-cost materials like perovskites for photovoltaic cells.

The study, published in Nature Energy, was led by Akshay Rao, a postdoctoral associate at Cornell's Sibley School of Mechanical and Aerospace Engineering. Rao and his team used machine learning to develop a new algorithm to optimize the layout of solar panels on a given piece of land.

The algorithm considers several factors, such as the amount of sunlight a particular location receives, the type of terrain, and the presence of obstacles like trees or buildings. As a result, the algorithm can produce a layout that maximizes the amount of power that can be produced from a particular piece of land by considering all of these considerations. The algorithm was tested on various real-world scenarios, and the results showed that it could lower the cost of solar energy by up to 20%. This is a significant improvement and could help make solar energy more affordable for everyone.

The research, which is the first to demonstrate how machine learning can be used to reduce solar energy costs, might significantly affect the renewable energy sector. The science of machine learning is expanding quickly, and it has the potential to completely change how we produce and utilize energy.

Improving Battery Technologies

Next-Generation Batteries Will Be Brought to You by AI

Addionics, a company that specializes in developing advanced battery technology, has announced that it will be using artificial intelligence (AI) to develop its next generation of batteries. The company believes that AI will allow it to produce more efficient, longer-lasting, and cheaper batteries. Addionics has been working with AI for several years. Addionics is certain that the technology will enable it to produce batteries uniquely suited to each client's requirements. For example, a customer who needs a battery for a car that will be used in a cold climate would be able to specify that they need a battery that can withstand cold temperatures.

Addionics believes AI will also allow it to create more efficient batteries than those currently on the market. The company is currently working on a new type of lithium-ion battery that it believes will be able to store more energy than current lithium-ion batteries. Addionics is also working on a new type of solid-state battery that it believes to store even more energy than its lithium-ion battery.

Addionics is not the only company that is using AI to develop batteries. Tesla, Panasonic, and LG are all using AI to develop batteries for their electric vehicles. AI is also being used to develop batteries for other applications, such as storing energy from solar panels and wind turbines.

A significant change in how batteries are made is the application of AI in their development. In the past, batteries were developed through trial and error. This was a time-consuming and expensive process. With AI, batteries can be developed much faster and cheaper.

The use of AI to develop batteries will likely lead to a major increase in the number of battery-powered devices on the market. This will increase the demand for battery materials, such as lithium and cobalt.

Societal Obligations

Utilities are critical infrastructures in any society and are expected to adhere to certain standards of conduct. As public service providers, these companies must meet their consumers' needs while maintaining transparency. Customers must be assured that their data is protected and that the utility company is working to reduce their carbon footprint.

The world is growing closer together. The interconnectedness of the population has created new challenges for society. Growing societal awareness of the importance of sustainability has also highlighted the necessity for ethical enterprises to participate actively in the sustainability movement. Businesses must now more than ever assume social responsibility as participants in their communities and have a constructive influence. To do so, they must understand the needs of their stakeholders and how they fit into the bigger picture of society.

The rapid adoption of distributed energy resources is forcing utilities to evolve from centralized energy providers to enablers of a more diversified, distributed energy system. As the utility industry goes through this transformation, the sector must be socially responsible. This is particularly important for investor-owned utilities, which exist for the benefit of their shareholders.

Social Inequity

Clean energy is a broad term that refers to any non-polluting, sustainable, or environmentally friendly energy source. This includes solar, wind, hydro, geothermal, or tidal energy. Investing in clean energy has several advantages, and the sooner we can all switch to this kind of energy, the better off we will all be. Sadly, investing in sustainable energy often costs more than using conventional fossil fuels. The good news is that the cost of clean energy will most likely decrease as we continue to research and develop new technologies. However, the transition toward clean energy also has the potential to create social inequity. Wealthier households will likely have easier access to clean energy sources than lower-income households. What can be done to ensure everyone has access to clean energy?

Adopting clean energy is frequently seen as a positive social development since it lowers carbon emissions, diversifies energy sources, and enhances public health by reducing air pollution. However, clean energy can exacerbate social inequities if not designed to empower all consumers. Policymakers and program designers can prevent this by involving various stakeholders in decision-making. Additionally, they can ensure that low-income and disadvantaged consumers have access to the benefits of clean energy.

Governments everywhere need to do more to reduce the wealth disparity and offer everyone a chance to profit from the clean energy economy. To do this, we must work to ensure that the benefits and opportunities of the clean energy economy are available to all and do not disproportionately benefit a few.

SDG&E's Community Impact Platform

The San Diego Gas & Electric Company's (SDG&E) Community Impact Platform was awarded the CIO 100 award in 2022 by IDG's CIO magazine. This award recognized SDG&E's innovative use of technology, specifically in deploying artificial intelligence to enhance their service and support a more sustainable and equitable energy future.

"The CIO 100 award recognizes the top 100 organizations using information technology in innovative ways to create business value," said Sarah Fister Gale, Executive Editor of CIO magazine and Conference Chair of the CIO 100 Symposium. "This year's winners are using technology to improve customer experiences, drive revenue growth and increase operational efficiency."

The Community Impact Platform is a digital platform that allows customers to see their energy choices' social, environmental, and economic benefits. In addition, the platform offers clients a simple method to learn about and engage in initiatives like solar, electric vehicle charging, and energy efficiency that has positively impacted the neighborhood. "We are honored to be recognized by CIO magazine as a leader in using technology to create social and economic value," said Scott Drury, SDG&E's Senior Vice President of Innovation and Technology. "The Community Impact Platform is a great example of how we use technology to empower our customers to make a difference in the community."

The Community Impact Platform was launched in 2018 and has earned several awards, including a CIO 100 award, a Green IT Award from the US Green Chamber of Commerce, and a Climate Change Business Journal Award.

Tech for Good Initiatives

Many of the world's largest power producers invest in technology and research to help the planet and their bottom lines. For example, a power plant in the US Midwest teamed up with an agricultural co-op to test a wind turbine that would produce power only when winds were at a certain speed. The turbines would shut off when winds were too strong to prevent damage to nearby crops.

As climate change becomes more pressing, so does the need for more sustainable energy sources. While solar, wind, and other technologies can help reduce emissions and meet increasing demand, they also require extensive hardware and maintenance. These high up-front costs are often a barrier to entry for many communities. What if there was a way to significantly reduce the cost of entry to these green energy sources? Blockchain technology has the potential to do just that. With a decentralized network that records data, transfers value, and maintains integrity, there is potential to reduce costs for energy suppliers and consumers. This reduction could stem from increased efficiency, reduced need for intermediaries, and enhanced transparency. However, the extent of cost savings will depend on the specific implementation and operational factors. Further research and case studies are necessary to substantiate these potential benefits.

It is estimated that data-driven load management could save the US electricity sector up to $20 billion annually. For example, customers' thermostats can be remotely adjusted to accommodate peak electricity consumption, or incentives can be provided to encourage the installation of energy-efficient LED lighting. Utility companies may also collaborate with independent technology vendors to offer a range of data-driven home energy enhancements, including smart water heaters, smart plugs, and smart outlets. These innovations allow utilities to remotely manage customer electricity demand, which can be beneficial during high-usage periods.

Rising to the Call

Smart grids, electric vehicles, and home solar panels are just a few ways the utility industry is changing to meet customer needs. Customers are demanding cleaner, more reliable, and more efficient energy sources. Utility providers who can adapt to these client needs will be able to compete in the ever-evolving market. For example, we are currently witnessing an increase in the number of utilities supplying solar panels to their consumers, thanks to growing knowledge of the advantages of solar energy. In addition, these products are now profitable for utilities as they can sell solar panels at a price lower than their cost of generating electricity from conventional sources thanks to the falling costs of solar panels. With the rise in utility offerings, we can expect a greater influx of solar power soon.

Key Takeaways

- Utilities are going toward NetZero and are at the center of the energy transition. They also have a greater social responsibility.

- Clean energy regulations will get considerably stricter; businesses and individuals must prepare in advance.

- Decreasing the cost of renewable energy will increase the prosumers, and organizations will be keen to embrace clean energy. Citizen consciousness will evaluate organizations based on their commitment to sustainability.

CHAPTER 6

Generating Power in the New Low Carbon Economy

The world is rapidly changing regarding how it generates and uses energy. A new low-carbon economy is emerging with growing concerns about climate change and the need for sustainable energy sources. This new economy is focused on reducing carbon emissions and increasing the use of clean energy sources. Generating power in the new low-carbon economy is becoming increasingly important as the world transitions away from fossil fuels. This chapter will provide an overview of the challenges and opportunities associated with generating power in the new low-carbon economy and how technology can help with this journey.

Introduction

The development of solar cells brought about a shift in how energy is produced. This change would iterate in the hands of various physicists and engineers over hundreds of years. The history of solar energy is a fascinating story of innovation and progress.

© Debashish Roy 2024
D. Roy, *AI for Utilities*, https://doi.org/10.1007/979-8-8688-0202-7_6

Solar energy is nothing new. People have used solar power as far back as the 7th century B.C. Energy from the sun has been treasured and used in its most basic forms for almost as long as there have been people on the planet. The sun's energy was first harnessed by using a magnifying glass to concentrate it so that fires could be started for cooking. By the 3rd century B.C., Greeks and Romans bounced sunlight off "burning mirrors" to light sacred torches for religious ceremonies.

Ancient civilizations used sunrooms to harness the sun's natural warmth. These usually south-facing rooms have captured and concentrated sunlight from the famous Roman bathhouses to Native American abodes and are still popular in many modern homes.

One legend in Greek solar history is of the scientist Archimedes setting fire to besieging wooden ships from the Roman Empire. According to legend, he used bronze shields to reflect sunlight, concentrating its rays to attack the enemy before they reached land.

Think of it as an ancient solar laser beam. Whether this happened in Archimedes' time or not is unverified. But this experiment in solar power was tested by the Greek navy in the 1970s. They set fire to a wooden test ship 50 meters away using nothing but the legendary bronze shield and solar light energy.

Albert Einstein had a role to play in bringing the world's attention to solar energy and its potential. In 1905, Einstein published a paper on the photoelectric effect and how light carries energy. Einstein's paper on the photoelectric effect in 1905 is titled "On a Heuristic Viewpoint Concerning the Production and Transformation of Light." In this paper, Einstein proposed a photoelectric effect theory explaining light carries energy and how it can be used to eject electrons from a metal surface. This theory was based on the idea that the energy of light is carried by individual particles called photons, which transfer their energy to the electrons when they collide. Einstein's theory could explain various observed phenomena not accounted for by previous theories and laid the foundation for the development of quantum mechanics. This generated more attention and acceptance for solar power on a broader scale.

The big leap toward solar cells like the ones used in panels today came from the work of Bell Labs in 1954. Three scientists there, Daryl Chapin, Calvin Fuller, and Gerald Pearson, created a more practical solar cell using silicon.

Scientists and engineers are committed to solar as a leading source of clean, affordable electricity for everyone. And they have made significant advancements in solar technology over the years. This has helped the world move away from conventional energy generation based on fossil fuels like coal, oil, and natural gas, which currently account for 80% of the world's energy generation. Unfortunately, they are also the primary human source of greenhouse gas emissions.

Utilities are on a countdown to reinvention. Self-generation will become a viable alternative for everyone when residential solar and battery storage systems become widely available and affordable, bringing the cost of off-grid energy on par with that of centralized electricity. Unlocking the value through optimizing connected distributed energy resources and avoiding some of the additional generation and infrastructure costs required can deliver significant financial, network, and societal benefits.

Generation Infrastructure Planning

Recently there has been an increased focus on using AI for power generation infrastructure planning. This is due to the several advantages that AI may offer, including increased effectiveness, precision, and scalability. One of the main benefits of using AI for power generation infrastructure planning is the improved accuracy that it can provide. This is because AI can consider many different variables and data points that human planners might not be able to. In addition, AI can constantly learn and update its models as new data becomes available, providing more accurate planning over time.

Scalability is another advantage of utilizing AI for planning power generation infrastructure. This is because AI can handle many data points and factors, which allows it to be used for planning on a large scale. AI may also be utilized to automate numerous planning-related processes, increasing productivity even more. Overall, AI has many benefits for power generation infrastructure planning. AI can provide improved accuracy, efficiency, and the ability to scale. These benefits can help improve the planning of power generation infrastructure, ultimately leading to improved outcomes.

Artificial intelligence is currently used in the energy sector to improve the reliability of power grids, monitor the performance of power plants, address the challenge of fluctuating demand, reduce energy costs through smart meters, and enable more efficient energy usage through thermostats that adapt to household schedules. Smart meters, with their advanced data collection, storage, and analysis capabilities, allow utilities to offer consumers a broader range of energy management products and services.

In addition, robots and drones are employed for power plant inspections using artificial intelligence. While this may not directly lead to more efficient energy production, it does contribute to more efficient plant operations by reducing unplanned downtimes and ensuring timely maintenance. This, in turn, helps maintain consistent energy output and prolongs the life of power plant equipment.

Maximizing Value of Power Generating Assets

The objective of a power plant is to generate electricity while maximizing asset value. Numerous elements, such as the cost of operation, the equipment's dependability, efficiency, and environmental impact, affect the value of the assets. In the past, power plants were operated using manual controls. The operator would modify the equipment based on their experience and the readings from the various sensors in the plant. This approach was often reactive, meaning the operator would make changes after the asset was not performing optimally. It also was labor-intensive and required significant skill and expertise from operators to ensure the safe and efficient operation of the power plant.

Over time, technological advancements led to the development of computer-based control systems that automate many tasks previously performed manually. These control systems allow for greater precision and consistency in the operation of power plants and reduce the need for manual intervention, leading to improved efficiency and safety.

Today, many power plants, mostly those in Asia, use a combination of manual and computer-based control systems, with the latter providing advanced monitoring and control capabilities. With the development of increasingly sophisticated technologies, the trend toward automation in the power generation industry will likely continue, using artificial intelligence in all systems.

Boiler Turbine Generators (BTG) are one of the crucial systems of a power plant operation. BTG can be either manual or automatic systems. In the past, many BTG systems were operated manually, where operators would physically adjust various systems and equipment to regulate power generation. This method of operation was labor-intensive and required significant skill and expertise from operators to ensure the safe and efficient operation of the power plant.

Today, however, many BTG systems are automated using computer-based control systems. These control systems allow for greater precision and consistency in the operation of power plants and reduce the need for manual intervention, leading to improved efficiency and safety. For example, in an automated BTG system, the control system monitors various parameters, such as steam pressure and temperature, and adjusts the operation of the boilers, turbines, and generators accordingly.

Predictive analytics may now be used to control power plants because of the advancements in artificial intelligence (AI). AI can take in data from various sensors in the plant and use that data to predict how the asset will perform in the future. Based on this prediction, the AI can adjust the equipment to maximize the asset's value.

For instance, if the AI anticipates that an asset will become less dependable, the AI can modify the machinery to lessen the effects of the asset's downtime. Or, if the AI predicts that an asset will be more efficient in the future, the AI can make changes to maximize the output of the asset.

The benefits of using AI to operate power plants are numerous. AI can assist power plants to prevent production loss, reduce downtime, and increase efficiency by adjusting the equipment based on forecasts. In addition, AI can help power plants reduce their environmental impact by modifying the equipment that minimizes the release of emissions.

Overall, AI is a powerful tool that can be used to maximize the value of power-generating assets. AI can assist power plants in avoiding expensive issues and increasing overall efficiency by forecasting the future performance of the assets.

Carbon Optimization

Carbon optimization during power generation using AI is a process whereby the carbon output of a power plant is monitored and controlled to minimize emissions. This is accomplished by tracking and real-time adjusting carbon dioxide output levels using sensors and algorithms. Reduced greenhouse gas emissions, improved air quality, and climate change mitigation are all advantages of this process. In the past, carbon optimization during power generation was a manual process that was often error-prone and time-consuming. However, with the advent of AI, this process can now be automated and carried out with much greater accuracy and efficiency.

One of the key benefits of employing AI for carbon optimization is recognizing and addressing issues in real time. For example, if a power plant emits too much carbon dioxide, the AI system can immediately adjust the output levels to bring them back to the desired level. Compared to the previous manual approach, which frequently caused delays of several hours or even days before the issue was fixed, this is a considerable improvement. Another advantage of using AI for carbon optimization is that it can help to predict future trends. As a result, the power plant's output can be adjusted using this knowledge in advance, reducing emissions before they even happen. Overall, using AI for carbon optimization during power generation using AI is a highly effective way to reduce emissions and help mitigate climate change. It is also much more efficient and accurate than the old manual system, making it an essential tool for the future of sustainable energy.

Key Takeaways

- Traditional power generation ideas are evolving, and finding new ways to generate cleaner energy is now more critical than ever. Digitalization of power plants is inevitable, and AI will play a significant role in it.

- Power generation assets are getting challenged by the increased load and age. AI is bringing in new ways.

- Carbon balancing is a fine art, and AI will help with that significantly.

CHAPTER 7

Microgrid – Macro Impact

The development and deployment of microgrids have had a profound effect on the global energy landscape. The emergence of distributed energy resources (DERs) has enabled distributed electricity generation and consumption, creating new opportunities for energy production and consumption efficiency, providing grid-level services to support grid reliability, and offering the possibility of a low-carbon, resilient, and secure energy system. This chapter will explore the macro-level impacts of microgrids, including economic, environmental, and social considerations and AI and advanced technology applications in this space.

Introduction

A strong winter storm that hit Texas on February 11, 2021, started the state-wide power outage. The storm severely damaged the state's electric grid and caused extensive power outages. More than 4 million customers lost power, and nearly 200,000 were still without power as of February 16. The outages left many Texans without heat or running water and caused at least 26 deaths. Hospitals, nursing homes, and other critical facilities were forced to rely on backup generators, and some ran out of fuel. The storm also disrupted the state's natural gas and water systems, causing widespread shortages. Many Texans were forced to boil their water to make it safe to drink. The storm caused an estimated $195 million in damage to the state's electric grid. In addition, there were significant repercussions from the state's infrastructural failures and power outages. The storm compelled the closure of government buildings, businesses, and schools. The outages also left many Texans without heat or running water and caused widespread disruptions to the state's water and natural gas systems.

In many parts of the world, power outages are a regular occurrence. They can be caused by severe weather, problems with the electrical grid, or other factors. A microgrid is a compact, localized energy system that can power a restricted region during a power outage. Microgrids are gaining popularity as reliable sources of power during outages. They are environmentally friendly since they are frequently powered by renewable energy sources like solar and wind.

In addition, microgrids can be used to power critical infrastructure during an outage, such as hospitals and emergency services. There are many benefits to using microgrids during power outages. They can provide power to a small area without relying on a large, centralized power plant, offering greater flexibility and resilience. While microgrids can be more efficient in certain contexts – such as reducing transmission losses by generating power closer to where it's used – their efficiency compared to traditional power plants can vary depending on factors like technology and scale. Additionally, microgrids produce no emissions when utilizing renewable energy sources, and building them is generally less expensive than constructing traditional power plants.

Microgrids are a potentially effective way to deal with the issue of power disruptions. Compared to conventional power plants, they are more cost-effective to develop, efficient, and ecologically friendly. Compared to conventional grid-tied systems, microgrids offer a variety of advantages, such as higher energy security, improved dependability, and increased power generation and distribution flexibility. Microgrids can also help reduce greenhouse gas emissions by enabling renewable energy sources and providing more efficient power generation and distribution.

Eliminating Energy Poverty and Bringing Equality

Microgrids can help to eliminate energy poverty and bring equality to communities that the traditional grid has long underserved. Microgrids can help dramatically cut families' and businesses' energy costs when used with energy-saving techniques. In the face of power outages and severe weather, microgrids can help communities become more resilient. Microgrids can also contribute to developing more regional and sustainable energy systems because they can be tailored to a community's unique demands.

Tackling Energy Poverty in Nigeria Through Artificial Intelligence

When it comes to energy poverty, Nigeria is one of the most affected countries in the world. With a population of over 200 million people, the majority of whom live in rural areas, Nigeria has one of the lowest electrification rates in the world. In fact, only about 40% of the population has access to electricity. This lack of access to electricity has a huge impact on the lives of Nigerians. It limits economic opportunities, as businesses cannot operate without power, and it reduces the quality of life, as people cannot cook or study at night. In addition, energy poverty greatly impacts health, as people cannot keep vaccines cold or use life-saving medical equipment. However, there is hope that Nigeria can overcome energy poverty with the help of artificial intelligence (AI). AI is helping to identify and target areas of the country most in need of electrification. AI can also help optimize energy production and distribution, so everyone can access electricity. Nigeria has the potential to overcome energy poverty and improve the lives of its people with the power of AI.

The rapid population growth in Nigeria has increased the overreliance on fossil fuels that contributed to socioeconomic drawbacks. The massive demand and the lack of an established energy supply chain in Nigeria resulted in acute energy poverty. In 2020, the Rural Electrification Agency (REA) estimated that almost 90 million people in Nigeria do not have access to grid electricity. The millions of those connected to the grid have less than 12 hours of electricity every day.

Advancing Economic, Racial, and Environmental Equity

The Sustainable Development Goals (SDGs) of the UN offer a comprehensive and widely accepted framework for considering the most critical issues the world is facing today and how to address them. Goal number 11, "Make cities and human settlements inclusive, safe, resilient and sustainable," is particularly relevant to the work of the Urban Institute's Justice Policy Center, which seeks to reduce crime and incarceration while promoting opportunity and fairness. In support of Goal 11, the Justice Policy Center is partnering with the Urban Institute's Center on Nonprofits and Philanthropy and the Technology and Innovation in the Public Sector program to develop and test a model that uses artificial intelligence (AI) and microgrid technology to help communities advance economic, racial, and environmental equity. The underlying idea of the concept is that while microgrids can supply communities with the energy they require to power their homes and businesses and increase resilience in the face of catastrophic weather events, AI can be used to detect and focus resources on regions of most need.

The project is piloted in two communities in the United States: Detroit, Michigan, and New Orleans, Louisiana. In each community, the project team works with local partners to identify areas of greatest need and develop plans for deploying AI and microgrid technology. The project is still in its early stages, but the team is already seeing promising results. For example, in Detroit, the team is working with Housing and Revitalization Department, using AI to identify vacant and abandoned properties that could be redeveloped into housing or commercial space. The plan is to power these vacant and abandoned spaces with microgrids. In New Orleans, the team uses AI to identify blighted properties that could be redeveloped into green space. The team also works with local partners to develop plans for deploying microgrids in both communities.

Electrifying Remote Places

In many remote places worldwide, people still do not have access to electricity. This is often due to a lack of infrastructure, which can be expensive and difficult to build in these areas. New technology, however, can assist in bringing electricity to these remote places. Microgrids are one of these technologies. Microgrids are small, localized power grids that can provide electricity to a small area. They are often used in rural or remote areas where it is not possible to connect to the main power grid. Another technology that can be used to electrify remote places is artificial intelligence (AI). AI can be used to manage and improve the operation of microgrids as well as to assist in their planning and construction. This can ensure that they are as effective as possible and that the demands of the local population are met. Together, microgrids and AI can be used to electrify even the most remote places in the world. This can improve the quality of life for people in these areas and provide them access to the modern world.

Electrifying Remote Indian Village

In a remote village in India, electrification has been a challenge. Traditional kerosene lamps, which are not only expensive but also unhealthy, have been used in the community for lighting. However, the village has a good amount of sunshine, so a microgrid powered by solar

113

panels and batteries is a viable option. The microgrid is designed such that it can be operated with minimal human intervention. It is equipped with sensors and an AI system that can predict the load on the grid and adjust the output accordingly. Additionally, the system can detect faults and take necessary actions to fix those faults. The villagers are very happy with the new system. They no longer have to worry about kerosene lamps and have access to reliable and affordable electricity.

Improving Power Quality Index

There are several ways that microgrids can help to raise the power quality index. One way is by providing a more reliable and consistent power supply. This can help to reduce or eliminate power outages and brownouts, which can cause major disruptions to businesses and households. Another way microgrids can improve the power quality index is by providing cleaner and more efficient energy. This can help to reduce pollution and carbon emissions and can also help to save money on energy costs.

Improving Equitable Grid Reliability

Microgrids are a promising solution for improving grid reliability, particularly in regions where the grid is vulnerable to weather-related disruptions. Microgrids can be created to run independently from the grid, acting as a backup power supply when the primary grid is down. In addition, microgrids can be equipped with smart grid technologies, such as advanced sensors and artificial intelligence (AI), to help optimize power generation and distribution. Artificial intelligence (AI) can be used to forecast demand trends and instantly improve microgrid operations. For example, AI-enabled sensors can monitor grid conditions and adjust power generation and distribution to meet demand. This can help avoid outages and ensure that power is delivered reliably and efficiently.

In addition, microgrids can be used to support the integration of renewable energy sources, such as wind and solar, into the grid. Microgrids can store excess energy generated by renewables when demand is low and release it when demand is high. This can help to balance the grid and improve its overall reliability. Microgrids are versatile solutions that can be tailored to the specific needs of each community. Microgrids can offer a dependable and resilient power source and enhance the grid's integration of renewable energy when used in conjunction with AI.

Investing for a Greener Future

Microgrids can play an important role in modernizing the power grid by improving reliability, efficiency, and sustainability and enabling the integration of clean energy sources and other advanced technologies. Microgrids are considered a solution to grid modernization for several reasons:

1. **Increased reliability and resilience**: Microgrids can operate independently from the main grid and provide backup power during outages, improving the reliability and resilience of the power supply.

2. **Improved energy efficiency**: Microgrids can optimize local renewable energy sources, reducing the need for energy imports and increasing energy efficiency.

3. **Enhanced grid flexibility**: Microgrids can support the integration of renewable energy sources, electric vehicles, and other distributed energy resources into the grid, enhancing its flexibility and adaptability.

4. **Better integration of renewable energy**: Microgrids can facilitate the deployment of renewable energy sources in remote or underserved communities, enabling the integration of clean energy into the grid.

5. **Improved security and control**: Microgrids can provide a secure and controllable power supply, reducing dependence on the main grid and providing more localized control over the energy system.

Renewable microgrids are appealing because they offer a range of benefits that improve energy security, reduce costs, and enhance sustainability for communities. Renewable microgrids are typically owned and controlled by local entities, allowing for more localized decision-making and control over the energy system. They can operate independently from the main grid and provide backup power during outages, improving the reliability and resilience of the power supply. Also, renewable microgrids can rely on clean, renewable energy sources, such as solar or wind power, reducing the community's dependence on fossil fuels and improving air quality. In addition, renewable microgrids can reduce energy costs for communities by reducing dependence on imported energy and utilizing local renewable energy sources. Lastly, renewable microgrids can provide communities with greater energy independence and security, reducing dependence on external energy sources and improving energy security.

Microgrids can provide many benefits to both the electric grid and the environment. One benefit of microgrids is that they can help increase the electric grid's resilience. For example, when there is a power outage, a microgrid can disconnect from the primary grid and operate independently. This can help to prevent blackouts from spreading throughout the grid.

Another benefit of microgrids is that they can help to reduce carbon emissions. Renewable energy-powered microgrids can aid in replacing fossil fuels and cutting greenhouse gas emissions. In addition, microgrids can help to increase the efficiency of the electric grid by reducing line losses.

Microgrids are a smart investment for a greener future. Microgrids can help increase the electric grid's resilience and reduce carbon emissions. In addition, microgrids can help to increase the efficiency of the electric grid.

Integrating Microgrid with Energy Ecosystem

The traditional grid is a centralized system that delivers electricity from a handful of large power plants to millions of customers. The grid is an aging system vulnerable to weather, cyberattacks, and other disruptions. A microgrid is a decentralized system that generates, stores, and manages its power. Microgrids can be powered by renewable energy sources, such as solar and wind, or by conventional sources, such as natural gas. Microgrids are more resilient than the traditional grid because they can island themselves from the grid and continue to operate during a grid outage. Microgrids can also provide grid stability by responding to real-time fluctuations.

The traditional grid is a one-way system that delivers electricity from power plants to customers. Microgrids are two-way systems that can send electricity back to the grid when needed. Microgrids can help utilities meet their renewable energy goals by providing a way to integrate renewable energy into the grid. Microgrids can also provide grid stability and resiliency, becoming increasingly important as the grid becomes more complex. Utilities are beginning to recognize the value of microgrids and are starting to invest in them. In the future, microgrids will become an integral part of the energy ecosystem, providing a cleaner, more reliable, and more resilient power system.

Key Takeaways

- Microgrid is a solution that has the potential to tackle both energy poverty and clean energy mission.

- One way to provide remote communities with clean, affordable, and reliable electricity is through microgrids. Microgrids are small-scale energy systems that can operate independently from the traditional grid. They can be powered by renewable energy sources like solar and wind providing a more reliable and cost-effective energy solution for remote communities.

- Investing in microgrid technologies will help bring energy security and improve the overall reliability of the power system.

- Sophisticated AI solutions will help embrace, adopt, and integrate microgrid solution with the overall energy ecosystem.

CHAPTER 8

Intelligent Transmission and Distribution

The dawn of the 21st century has seen tremendous advancement in the field of technology, and the introduction of artificial intelligence (AI) has only accelerated the rate of innovation. In particular, the application of AI to the transmission and distribution of electricity has been a game changer in terms of efficiency, safety, and reliability. This chapter will discuss the potential applications of AI in the transmission and distribution of electricity and the implications for the industry's future. Specifically, the chapter will explore how AI can optimize electricity transmission and distribution, including predictive maintenance, dynamic demand response, and autonomous grid operation. Additionally, the chapter will examine the challenges associated with using AI in transmission and distribution networks and the steps that must be taken to ensure successful implementation.

Introduction

In 1882, Thomas Edison opened America's first power plant at Pearl Street Station in lower Manhattan, serving just 59 customers. Since then, the customer base across the utility industry has grown to hundreds of

© Debashish Roy 2024
D. Roy, *AI for Utilities*, https://doi.org/10.1007/979-8-8688-0202-7_8

millions. However, the overall structure of the industry – comprising a vast network of approximately 5800 power plants, over 2.7 million miles of power lines, and numerous distribution centers – has not undergone significant modernization.

High costs for infrastructure and distribution lines, as well as stringent governmental regulations, naturally create opportunities for monopolies to develop in the market. As a result, three separate US grids produce and transmit power under the mandate to provide low-cost, reliable energy as a public good.

In the United States, the average age of power plants is over 30 years, and of power, transformers are over 40 years. According to the federal task force charged with its investigation, this deteriorating transmission system led to the 2003 Northeast blackout, the largest failure in US history. It left 50 million people without power for several days when an overloaded transmission line sagged and struck a tree. These incidents can ripple and impact the entire area grid and are challenging for utility providers to handle. In addition, the growth of distributed production, in which individual users produce and utilize their electricity from renewable sources like wind and solar, presents another difficulty. Due to the complicated nature of supply and demand, utility companies are compelled to purchase excess energy from individual consumers who produce more power than they consume and transmit the extra energy back to the system. Since 2010, solar use has more than tripled, and this trend is poised to continue as photovoltaic cells, the devices that generate electricity from sunlight, decrease in cost and increase in efficiency.

The current system was not built to accommodate this diversification in energy sources, especially not the rise in renewable resources. Instead, when demand outpaces supply, utilities turn on backup fossil fuel-powered plants, known as 'peaker plants,' at a minute's notice to avoid a cascading catastrophe. This procedure is the most expensive and wasteful part of business for these companies, manifesting in higher electricity bills for consumers and enhanced greenhouse gas emissions into the atmosphere. These problems will be exacerbated as the US energy demand is projected to increase steadily.

The smart grid is a system that uses information technology to manage electricity delivery from generation sources to consumers. The smart grid includes a variety of technologies and systems that work together to provide a more reliable, efficient, and environmentally friendly electricity system. However, the smart grid still needs to be intelligent. The current smart grid is limited in its ability to self-diagnose problems, make decisions, and adapt to changing conditions. An intelligent smart grid could do all these things and more. AI can help to make the smart grid more intelligent. AI can be used to create a virtual power plant that can predict demand and supply, optimize the use of resources, and provide real-time feedback to users. AI can also be used to create smart meters that can provide detailed information about electricity usage and help identify potential problems. Transitioning from a smart grid to an intelligent smart grid will require a significant investment of time and money. However, the benefits of an intelligent smart grid will be well worth the investment.

AI will be the brain of this future smart grid. To quickly decide how to effectively allocate energy resources, the system will continuously gather and synthesize enormous volumes of data from millions of smart sensors across the country. Additionally, the advances made from 'deep learning' algorithms, a system where machines learn independently from spotting patterns and anomalies in large data sets, will revolutionize both the demand and supply side of the energy economy.

Asset Management

Electric utilities can manage important assets by using utility asset management, which keeps track of various factors like age, usage, maintenance history, and more. Asset performance management (APM) enhances asset management with data analytics, condition monitoring, and predictive maintenance to support better operational decisions. The risk of equipment failure is reduced while equipment life is optimized using a utility asset management system with APM capabilities. The results are seen in gained efficiency, lower emissions, and reduced costs, with maximum uptime and reliability of service for end users. However, utilities sit at the convergence of a technology revolution impacting both distributed and centralized assets, as well as complex business processes. When combined with the persistent challenges of aging infrastructure, an aging workforce, and increasing regulatory requirements, operational leaders need to reduce risk while improving financial performance and infrastructure resilience. This is achieved through the coordinated activity of an organization to realize value from its assets.

Intelligent Asset Analytics

Predicting the RUL (Remaining Useful Life) for an Asset

Utilities have the problem of preserving their current asset portfolio while offering good customer service with constrained resources worldwide. Asset management is critical to ensuring that utilities meet this challenge; however, cost-effective approaches for assessing asset condition, performance, and remaining service life are required. The current state of the art for estimating remaining life by applying several methodologies depends heavily on asset lifespan. There are many ways to predict the remaining useful life (RUL) of a utility asset using AI. Regression algorithms are frequently used to forecast the RUL based on historical performance data. Another strategy is constructing a decision tree to pinpoint the important variables affecting an asset's RUL. Both approaches have their advantages and disadvantages. Regression is a more mathematically complex approach, but it can be more accurate if the past performance data represents the future. Although decision trees are more understandable and sometimes simpler to read, they may be less accurate if the major variables that affect the RUL are not understood beforehand. Ultimately, the best approach to predicting the RUL of a utility asset using AI will depend on the specific data and circumstances. In general, however, either regression or a decision tree can be a helpful tool for making predictions about the RUL of an asset.

Producing Recommendations About Service or Maintenance

In recent years, there has been an increasing trend of using artificial intelligence (AI) to produce recommendations about the service or maintenance of utility assets.

The advantages of using AI in this context are numerous:

1. AI can help to identify patterns that may not be readily apparent to human analysts.

2. AI can process large amounts of data much more quickly than humans, meaning that more data can be considered when making recommendations.

3. AI can help improve the accuracy of recommendations by reducing certain human biases. However, it's important to note that bias can still be unintentionally introduced if the input data is not carefully designed and curated.

AI offers powerful tools for producing recommendations about the service and maintenance of utility assets by leveraging deep analytics to identify predictive variables for asset breakdowns. Instead of simply scheduling annual maintenance based on past patterns, AI can analyze complex data sets to predict when an asset is likely to fail. This allows for proactive, risk-based maintenance schedules that optimize asset performance and prevent unexpected breakdowns, rather than relying on fixed time-based intervals.

Another approach is to use AI to generate recommendations based on the specific needs of a particular asset. For example, if data indicates that a particular asset is consistently operating at below-optimal levels, AI can recommend that the asset be serviced or maintained to improve its performance.

AI is a powerful tool that can be used to produce recommendations about the service or maintenance of utility assets. The advantages of using AI in this context are numerous, and the different approaches that can be used to generate recommendations offer a great deal of flexibility. As such, AI is likely to play an increasingly important role in the future service and maintenance of utility assets.

Utility Pole Deterioration Modeling

The electric grid is one of the most important infrastructure systems in the United States. In addition, it is one of the most vulnerable, as evidenced by the recent major power disruptions brought on by hurricanes. The grid comprises millions of miles of wire, hundreds of thousands of transformers, and millions of poles and other structures. The poles are particularly important, as they support the wires that carry electricity from the power plants to our homes and businesses.

Utility poles are made of wood, concrete, or metal and can be as tall as 100 feet. As a result, they are constantly exposed to the elements, and over time, they can deteriorate. This can lead to the poles falling over, which can cause blackouts and other problems.

To prevent widespread outages, it is important to be able to predict which poles are most likely to fail. This is a challenging undertaking because a variety of factors, such as weather, insects, and pole age, can cause pole deterioration. Fortunately, there is a growing body of research on utility pole deterioration modeling using AI. This research is helping to create better models for predicting pole failure, which will ultimately help to keep the power grid running smoothly.

Long-Term Health Index Prediction for Power Asset

The long-term health index (LTHI) is a key performance indicator for power assets. It is a measure of an asset's ability to generate electricity over its lifetime and is used to predict the lifetime performance of the asset.

LTHI is influenced by several factors, including the asset's design, operating conditions, and maintenance regime. Unfortunately, many of these factors are difficult to predict or control, making it difficult to accurately forecast an asset's LTHI.

However, recent advances in artificial intelligence (AI) provide new ways to accurately predict an asset's LTHI. In addition, AI can be used to analyze data from various sources, including asset performance data, maintenance records, and weather data.

AI-based models can identify patterns and relationships that would be difficult to spot using traditional methods. This allows for more accurate predictions of an asset's LTHI.

Some companies are already using AI to predict the LTHI of power assets. This is likely to become more widespread as the technology develops and becomes more affordable.

Health Monitoring of Timber Utility Poles

The use of timber utility poles is widespread in the utility industry. The health of these poles is critical to the electrical grid's stability. AI can be used to monitor the health of these poles.

Artificial intelligence (AI) can be used to spot early degradation in wooden utility poles. This information can be used to plan maintenance and repairs before the pole fails. This can help to avoid power outages and keep the electrical grid stable.

AI can also be used to monitor the environment around the utility poles. The potential dangers that could harm the poles can be found using this information. Utilizing this knowledge will enable you to take precautions to protect the poles. In addition, AI can help to improve the safety and reliability of the electrical grid. This technology can help to save money and avoid power outages.

Assets Inspection Using Drone

The power transmission business will be transformed by the deployment of drones and AI for asset inspection. By using these technologies, inspectors can quickly and easily identify potential problems with power lines, towers, and other critical infrastructure.

Drones with high-resolution cameras and AI software can quickly scan large areas for potential problems. This can save inspectors substantial time and effort and allow them to focus on other tasks.

AI-driven software can also aid in detecting issues that might not be immediately obvious by analyzing data from various sources. By identifying patterns and potential dangers, AI can improve maintenance schedules and prevent potential outages. Moreover, this can be done at a scale that is not easily achievable by humans, thanks to the automation and processing power of AI.

The power transmission business is already demonstrating the value of asset assessment using drones and AI. As these technologies continue to develop, they are likely to have an even greater impact on the efficiency and safety of power transmission assets.

Benefits of Assets Inspection Using Drone

1. **Reducing risk and danger**: Using drones significantly improves worker safety. This is made even clearer in the case of buildings like oil and gas refineries, which feature a variety of dangerous situations like tight spaces, tall, intricate stacks and pipelines, toxic compounds, and locations with low oxygen levels. Reducing the human interaction required for such asset assessment significantly lowers the possibility of worker fatalities or injuries.

2. **Minimize downtime**: Since less scaffolding, towers, and other equipment need to be set up, surveillance can be completed more quickly. This not only reduces downtime and increases productivity but also allows for more frequent inspections, further enhancing operational efficiency.

3. **Lowered insurance premiums**: Removing the need for manual inspection reduces the cost of worker and inspector insurance. Additionally, it eliminates the need for pricey Health, Safety, and Environment (HSE) procedures.

Consumer Behavior

Smart Grid Consumer Behavioral Model

Smart grid consumer behavioral models use artificial intelligence (AI) to better understand and predict consumer behavior. These models can help utilities optimize the grid, reduce energy costs, and improve customer satisfaction.

Behavioral models can be used to understand various customer behaviors, including energy consumption, load shedding, and demand response. Analyzing historical data using AI-powered models can reveal patterns and trends in consumer behavior. This information can be used to develop predictions about future behavior.

Utilities can use behavioral models to develop targeted marketing and outreach programs. For example, a utility may use a model to identify customers likely to participate in a demand response program. The utility can then develop targeted marketing materials and programs to encourage these customers to participate.

Additionally, behavioral models can be employed to enhance grid operations. For example, a model may predict how customers will respond to a power outage. This information can be used to improve outage management and restoration plans.

Smart grid consumer behavioral models are a powerful tool for utilities. These models can help utilities reduce energy costs, improve customer satisfaction, and optimize grid operations.

Anomaly Detection Techniques in Advanced Metering Infrastructure

Anomaly detection techniques are used to find unusual or unexpected patterns in data. These techniques can be used to find equipment or systems problems, identify fraudulent activities, or detect other unusual behavior.

There are many different anomaly detection techniques, but some of the most common are machine learning, statistical analysis, and data mining. Machine learning is a type of artificial intelligence that can be used to find patterns in data. Statistical analysis can be used to identify unusual patterns by looking at the distribution of data. Data mining is a process of searching through data to find patterns.

Anomaly detection techniques are used in various industries, but they are significant in advanced metering infrastructure (AMI). AMI systems are used to measure and track electricity, water, and gas usage. In addition, these systems are used by utilities to manage resources and bill customers.

Anomaly detection techniques can be used to find problems with AMI systems. For example, if there is a sudden increase in electricity use, this could indicate a problem with the system. Anomaly detection can also be used to find fraudulent activities. For example, if someone uses a water meter to steal water, they will likely have a higher water usage than others in the same area.

Data mining is a particularly important anomaly detection technique for AMI systems. This is because AMI systems generate a large amount of data. This data can be used to find patterns that indicate problems with the system. For example, if there is a sudden increase in electricity use, this could indicate a problem with the system.

Anomaly detection techniques are important for AMI systems because they can help to find problems with the system. These techniques can also be used to find fraudulent activities. Data mining is a particularly important anomaly detection technique for AMI systems.

Household Characteristics from Electricity Meter Data

There is a lot of potential in using AI to understand household characteristics from electricity meter data. This data can be used to understand how a household uses energy, their appliances, and even their economic status.

Utilizing clustering algorithms is one approach within AI to better understand household characteristics. While clustering itself is a data analytics technique, when combined with AI, it can go further by not only grouping households with similar electricity usage patterns but also by predicting future behaviors, optimizing energy distribution, and tailoring services to different household types, such as those with high or low energy usage.

Another way AI can be utilized to understand household characteristics is through the use of classification algorithms. While classification itself is a data analytics technique, AI enhances this process by learning from large datasets and improving its predictions over time. For example, AI-driven classification algorithms can predict the types of appliances in a household based on electricity usage patterns. Beyond merely identifying energy-efficient or high-energy appliances, AI can provide insights into usage behaviors, optimize energy consumption, and suggest personalized energy-saving strategies.

Finally, regression algorithms can be used to understand the economic status of electricity meter data. This can be used to identify families that use more or less energy than usual, or those that are spending a lot of money on energy.

Building Load Prediction

In the past, predicting how much load a building would experience was a complex and inexact science. But with the advent of artificial intelligence (AI), it's now possible to create more accurate models that consider a variety of factors.

For example, the peak demand for a building can be predicted using historical data and weather trends by using artificial intelligence (AI). This information can be used to help utilities and building managers plan for increased demand and avoid blackouts or brownouts.

AI can also be used to monitor real-time data from sensors to identify trends and incipient problems. For example, suppose a sensor detects a sudden drop in water pressure. In that case, AI can automatically shut off water to non-essential areas of the building to prevent damage. In the future, AI will become even more important in managing buildings and their loads. For instance, AI will be necessary to control the intricate interconnections between these various systems as more buildings install solar panels and other renewable energy sources. However, as AI continues to evolve, the potential applications for building load prediction are limited only by our imagination.

Grid Security
Energy Theft Detection

Energy theft has been a problem for utilities for many years. With the advent of AI, energy theft detection is becoming much more sophisticated. AI can assist in identifying probable cases of energy theft and assisting in its prevention by analyzing patterns in energy usage. Meter manipulation is one of the most prevalent types of energy theft. This is when someone circumvents or illegally disconnects their meter to avoid paying for the energy they use. AI can help to identify meter tampering by analyzing patterns in energy usage. For example, if there is a sudden drop in energy usage, this could be an indication that someone has tampered with their meter.

Another form of energy theft is known as non-technical losses. Here the energy is lost due to faulty equipment or poor maintenance. AI can help to identify non-technical losses by analyzing patterns in energy usage. For example, if there is a sudden increase in energy usage, this could indicate a problem with the equipment.

AI can be used to detect energy theft in many ways. One is by analyzing the pattern of energy usage over time. If there is a sudden spike in usage, it could be an indication that someone is tampering with the meter. Another way is to use AI to compare the energy usage of similar buildings. If one building is using significantly more energy than others, it could be an indication of theft.

Energy theft is a serious problem that can significantly impact the energy costs. AI is a powerful tool that can be used to detect energy theft and help to reduce the cost of energy.

AI algorithms use energy consumption patterns, technical parameters of phase currents, neutral currents, voltages, power factors, and available smart meter events to identify where and how meter tampering is most likely to have occurred in cases where electricity thieves take steps to prevent energy consumption from being recorded. Significant decreases in usage often occur along with electrical anomalies when there are tampering tendencies. AI can be leveraged to tackle energy theft by analyzing large amounts of energy data to detect and prevent fraudulent electricity usage. This can be done through techniques such as:

1. **Anomaly detection**: AI algorithms can analyze electricity usage patterns to identify abnormal behavior, such as excessive usage during off-peak hours, which could indicate theft.

2. **Load profiling**: AI algorithms can create a profile of electricity usage for each consumer, which can then be used to identify suspicious behavior, such as significant changes in usage patterns.

3. **Image processing**: AI algorithms can process images captured by cameras to detect theft. For example, identifying the unauthorized connection of cables to electrical infrastructure.

4. **Predictive maintenance**: AI algorithms can predict equipment failure and prevent energy theft by detecting problems before they occur, reducing the likelihood of theft by exploiting these vulnerabilities.

Cyberattack Detection

The nation's critical infrastructure is under constant attack from various cyber adversaries. In response, the Department of Homeland Security (DHS) is turning to artificial intelligence (AI) to help defend our nation's utilities.

DHS's Science and Technology Directorate (S&T) is funding the development of a prototype system that uses AI to detect anomalies in utility data that could indicate a cyberattack. The Electric Infrastructure Security (EIS) Cyber-Attack Detection System, is being developed by a team of researchers from the University of Maryland, Argonne National Laboratory, and S&T.

The EIS system will use a variety of data sources, including control system data, power grid data, and weather data, to train a machine learning algorithm to detect anomalous behavior that could indicate a cyberattack. Additionally, the system will be designed to work in real time, providing alerts to utility operators so they can take action to mitigate the threat.

The EIS system is just one example of how AI is being used to defend our nation's critical infrastructure. S&T is also funding the development of AI-enabled systems to detect threats to the nation's water supply and to protect against cyberattacks on the electric grid. AI will become more crucial in keeping our critical infrastructure secure as the threat landscape changes.

Intrusion Detection System for Advanced Metering Infrastructure

An intrusion detection system (IDS) is a device or software application that monitors a network or system for malicious activity or policy violations. Any malicious activity or violation is reported to an administrator or collected centrally using a security information and event management

(SIEM) system. The outputs from many sources are combined by a SIEM system, which filters and analyzes the data using correlation techniques. IDS come in a variety of forms, including network-based IDS (NIDS), host-based IDS (HIDS), and application-based IDS (AIDS). NIDS monitors traffic on a network segment and analyzes it for suspicious activity. HIDS monitors activity on a single host, such as a server, and can be used to detect malicious activity, such as viruses or unauthorized access attempts.

To detect malicious activity, such as SQL injection attacks or cross-site scripting (XSS) attacks, Intrusion Detection Systems (IDS) are used to monitor activity within a particular application, such as a web server. SQL injection attacks involve inserting malicious SQL code into a query, allowing attackers to manipulate a database, while cross-site scripting attacks involve injecting malicious scripts into web pages viewed by other users, potentially stealing information or hijacking sessions.

In recent years, there has been increasing interest in using artificial intelligence (AI) for IDS. AI can perform various tasks, such as data pre-processing, feature selection, classification, and anomaly detection. AI-based IDS can improve the accuracy of detection by reducing the number of false positives (i.e., alerts not caused by malicious activity) and false negatives (i.e., malicious activity not detected by the IDS).

There are several different AI algorithms that can be used for IDS, including decision trees, rule-based systems, artificial neural networks, and support vector machines. IDS powered by AI are generally more accurate than traditional IDS but tend to be more sophisticated and resource intensive. As such, AI-based IDS are typically used in conjunction with traditional IDS to provide the best possible coverage.

False Data Injection Attacks in Power Systems

False data injection attacks in power systems involve attackers injecting misleading or incorrect data into the grid's monitoring systems. These attacks can disrupt the operation of the power grid by causing incorrect decisions, such as improper load balancing or triggering unnecessary shutdowns, leading to potential blackouts or equipment damage. As these attacks become more prevalent, AI can play a crucial role in detecting and preventing them by monitoring data for anomalies and suspicious activity. AI-based systems can identify patterns that indicate malicious behavior, allowing for swift responses to protect the integrity of the grid.

AI can help identify false data injection attacks by analyzing data for patterns and inconsistencies. For example, if data from a sensor shows a sudden increase in power usage, this could indicate an attack. AI is also capable of observing grid communications for indications of tampering. Preventing false data injection attacks requires real-time monitoring and analysis of data. AI can provide the speed and accuracy needed to detect attacks as they happen and take action to prevent them. Additionally, AI can help identify trends and vulnerabilities that attackers can exploit. By understanding these weaknesses, power companies can take steps to protect their systems.

False data injection attacks are a serious threat to the power grid. AI can help detect and prevent these attacks by monitoring data for anomalies and suspicious activity. By understanding the trends and vulnerabilities that attackers can exploit, power companies can take steps to protect their systems and keep the grid safe.

Communications and Security Management

Grid communications and security management is a process of handling communications and security for electric power grids. It involves using various technologies and protocols to ensure the grid's availability and security.

With the increasing complexity of electric power grids, there is a need for more sophisticated methods of managing communications and security. The application of artificial intelligence is one such strategy (AI). AI can be used to manage communications in many ways. For example, it can be used to monitor communications traffic to identify and isolate abnormal or unauthorized activity. It can also be used to automatically generate and distribute security updates to grid operators.

In addition, AI can be used to manage security for electric power grids. For example, it can be used, to keep an eye out for signals of hacking or attack on grid infrastructure. It can also be used to create and maintain security plans and procedures.

Overall, using AI can improve the efficiency and effectiveness of grid communications and security management. It can help to identify and resolve problems more quickly and can help to prevent or mitigate the impacts of disruptions and attacks.

Grid Resiliency

Harmonic Analysis in Power Distribution Networks

Harmonic analysis is the study of the waveforms of alternating current (AC) power. AI-powered harmonic analysis can be used in a power distribution network to find and fix issues brought on by harmonic currents. Harmonic currents can damage power distribution networks by overheating machinery and lowering the voltage. They can also cause interference with communication systems.

AI can be used to identify harmonic currents in a power distribution network. This information can correct the problem by re-routing the power or adding filters to the system.

AI-based harmonic analysis can assist in increasing the effectiveness of power distribution networks and preventing issues brought on by harmonic currents.

Fault Diagnosis of Smart Meters

In the past, electrical meters were read manually by meter readers who physically came to read the meter once a month. This process was not only time-consuming and costly, but it was also prone to human error.

With the advent of smart meters, this process has been automated. Smart meters communicate with the utility company via a wireless network and are read automatically.

However, even with this automation, some issues can still arise. One issue is that of false readings. Numerous factors, including meter tampering, radio interference, and even equipment failure, might cause this. Another issue is that of meter misreading. This can occur when the meter cannot properly communicate with the utility company or when there is an error in the meter itself.

To combat these issues, many utility companies are now turning to artificial intelligence (AI) for fault diagnosis of smart meters. AI can be used to detect false readings, and it can also be used to diagnose meter misreading.

One AI-based system that is being used for fault diagnosis is the Smart Meter Error Detection and Correction (SMEDAC) system. This system uses various algorithms to detect and correct errors in smart meter readings.

The Smart Meter Data Analytics and Visualization (SMDAV) system is another AI-based solution. This system uses data analytics to visualize smart meter data, and it can also be used to detect errors.

Utility providers are also using machine learning to diagnose smart meter faults. Machine learning is a type of AI that allows computers to learn from data.

One machine learning-based system is the Smart Meter Fault Detection and Isolation (SMFDI) system. This system employs several algorithms to find and isolate inaccuracies in readings from smart meters. As utility companies continue to adopt AI for fault diagnosis of smart meters, the accuracy of meter readings is expected to improve. This will ultimately lead to more reliable and accurate utility bills for customers.

Severity Analysis of Tree and Utility Pole Crashes (TUOP)

Electric utilities will use artificial intelligence to analyze weather conditions and improve the safety of their workers. They will also use data analytics to improve their maintenance activities. The AI-based tools will be used to predict and analyze the risk of falling trees or utility poles and reduce the risk of utility workers being injured or killed.

A research paper by the Pacific Northwest National Laboratory explores the potential of artificial intelligence for analyzing incidents involving tree and utility pole crashes to improve electric grid reliability. While trees can become hazards if they fall on power lines, causing outages or damage, utility poles are essential structures that support the power lines themselves. If a utility pole is damaged or removed, it can directly disrupt the grid's reliability. The study investigates how AI can help mitigate these risks by analyzing data to enhance the safety and stability of the electric grid.

This can be done using various pattern recognition algorithms like convolutional neural networks or support vector machines. The data needed for this analysis can be sourced from call center logs, social media, or crowdsourcing. Additionally, the information can be gathered manually by driving around areas and noting where trees and utility poles are located. This analysis can predict the risk of a crash at a particular location and suggest a maintenance schedule to avoid future crashes.

Emergency Response and Coordination

Electric utilities can now use artificial intelligence technology to automate emergency response and coordination, increasing efficiency and reducing costs.

Artificial intelligence can be used in electrical grid monitoring to provide early warning signs of emergencies. For example, an AI system can monitor grid data and search for patterns in the data to ascertain whether there is a chance of electrical surges or power outages. Once an emergency is declared, AI can be used to coordinate response efforts. For example, AI can monitor critical facilities such as hospitals or airports and shut off power if those systems are in danger. AI can also track down critical emergency information from media sources, such as the whereabouts of those needing help.

Artificial intelligence can help electric utilities in their disaster response and coordination using AI by analyzing data from sensors in the grid, weather reports, and other inputs to predict and prevent outages, track assets, and monitor critical infrastructure. With the increasing adoption of smart grids, utilities are generating massive amounts of data. AI is a perfect fit to analyze this data and provide actionable insights.

Here, the emphasis is on giving users access to real-time data analysis and information to facilitate quick decision-making in an emergency. The key here is to monitor, analyze, and react to changing conditions. These real-time solutions can be deployed on existing devices such as tablets and smartphones or used as part of a larger system. Again, the key here is to be able to monitor, analyze, and react to changing conditions.

Geographic Situational Awareness

Unsurprisingly, AI is starting to make a big impact on location-based services, and more and more people are discovering how AI can help them navigate their world. AI is playing a more prominent role in assisting you in making well-informed decisions about where to go and how to get there, from suggesting the finest travel locations to booking the best flights. AI can be used to analyze data and predict the best time to book a flight or whether a certain airport will likely experience delays. It can also be used to collect data about a location, such as weather patterns, cultural activities, and other events that might be happening. Then, a mobile app can offer suggestions for potential future travel destinations or assist you in making travel arrangements.

Artificial intelligence is now being used to help business decision-makers understand their customers' location and how it relates to their product or service offering. AI-powered data analysis can be used for this, or location-based data can be incorporated into current commercial software. AI is now being used to assist marketers in understanding the location of their customers and how it relates to their product or service offering. Businesses can improve the accuracy of their marketing initiatives by collecting information on the whereabouts of their clients. By analyzing data on customers' locations, marketers can better tailor their product or service offerings to meet the needs of their customers.

AI can transform the way a utility does business. It may be applied to automate tasks, predict client needs, and make data-driven decisions. Businesses are currently investigating the use of AI to enhance their operational procedures. For example, AI can be used to analyze data, collect signals, and generate visualizations to create situational awareness.

Key Takeaways

- Smarter and more connected – The network will be more responsive to real-time conditions and demands, making it more efficient and reliable.

- More renewable energy – A growing share of electricity will be generated from renewable sources, such as solar and wind.

- More electric vehicles – More electric vehicles on the road will mean more demand for electricity, which the network will need to be able to accommodate.

- More distributed generation – More electricity will be generated closer to where it is needed rather than at centralized power plants.

- Greater use of data, analytics, and AI – Data, analytics, and AI will be used increasingly to help manage the network and make it more efficient.

CHAPTER 9

Utilities Retail Reimagined

The way consumers interact with utility companies is changing rapidly, and AI is the driving force behind this transformation. Utilities Retail Reimagined using AI explores how AI is revolutionizing the retail side of utility companies, from customer service to energy consumption. We'll examine how AI impacts the customer experience and how companies leverage AI to optimize their operations and streamline customer engagement. We'll also explore how leading utilities are using AI-enabled solutions to transform customer engagement and drive customer loyalty. Finally, we'll discuss the implications of AI on the energy sector and what the future of utility retail looks like in an AI-driven world.

Introduction

The utility sector is undergoing a major technological transformation. Utilities find it challenging to hold on to customers and protect themselves against new distributed generation threats in highly competitive retail markets and traditionally regulated regimes. By digitizing the customer experience, utilities can simultaneously improve satisfaction and lower costs. Thanks to AI, utilities are positioned to take advantage of customer interest in deeper engagement. Utilities already have what AI needs to thrive on. They have a mountain of customer data. For machine learning

© Debashish Roy 2024
D. Roy, *AI for Utilities*, https://doi.org/10.1007/979-8-8688-0202-7_9

to operate or to be successful, it must have a cache of data to learn against. This is an unnatural advantage that they have that they are currently not exploiting or leveraging.

Empowering Customers

AI will be implemented to make customer service more efficient and effective. Customer service representatives can use AI to process data and respond to customers in real-time. AI can be used to monitor social media to identify customer issues, receive feedback, and suggest solutions. AI can also be used to automate processes like receiving orders from new clients, maintaining client information, and drafting service agreements. The use of pattern recognition, computer vision, and natural language processing enhances the utility experience. From switching to a new supplier to managing usage, customers are now given tools to help them navigate the utility experience. In the future, utilities are expected to invest in technologies to enable remote monitoring and management of critical infrastructure, such as power grids, water, and gas networks, etc.

Optimizing Customer–Agent Interactions with Natural Language Processing and Machine Learning

In the utility industry, customer–agent interactions are critical to providing excellent customer service. Utilities can improve customer satisfaction and cut operating costs by streamlining these interactions using natural language processing (NLP) and machine learning (ML). NLP can automatically extract customer information from unstructured text, such as emails, chat transcripts, and call notes. This data can then be utilized to direct consumers to the right agent, solve problems more quickly, and enhance self-service alternatives. ML can be used to predict customer needs and proactively offer solutions. For instance, using machine learning (ML), it is possible to spot trends in customer interactions that point to a high likelihood of churn. Utility companies can decrease customer attrition and raise customer satisfaction by proactively addressing these problems. In addition to NLP and ML, utilities can use data analytics to improve customer–agent interactions. Data analytics can be used to identify customer service issues, understand customer sentiment, and track customer interactions over time. Utilities may improve customer experiences by better understanding the facts underlying customer–agent interactions.

Conversational AI Chatbot in Energy Informatics

The use of Conversational AI chatbots in the utility industry has been on the rise in recent years. The chatbots are used to handle customer queries and complaints and to promote and sell products and services.

There are many advantages of using chatbots in the utility industry. The chatbots are available 24/7 and can handle a large number of queries at the same time. They are also able to provide personalized service and can remember customer preferences.

Another advantage of using chatbots is that they can help to reduce customer effort. The chatbot can assist customers who are having trouble paying their bills, for instance, by guiding them through the procedure. As a result, the customer may find it time- and frustration-saving. In addition, chatbots can help to improve customer satisfaction levels. This is because they can provide a quick and efficient service tailored to the customer's needs.

Some challenges need to be considered when using chatbots in the utility industry. For example, chatbots need to handle a high volume of queries and complaints. They also need to be able to understand the customer's needs and provide relevant information.

Overall, the use of chatbots in the utility industry has many advantages. Chatbots can provide a quick and efficient service that is tailored to the customer's needs. Additionally, they can aid in lowering consumer effort and raising customer satisfaction levels.

Distributed Machine Learning for Energy Trading

The environment for energy trading has drastically changed during the last two decades. The once-niche market has become increasingly globalized, with energy trading taking place on exchanges worldwide. At the same time, the advent of new technologies has allowed for the development of new trading strategies and the rise of new energy trading firms.

Energy trading companies have had to adapt to and adopt new technology to stay up with the constantly shifting environment. Distributed machine learning (DML) is one of the most significant technologies in recent years. DML is a form of artificial intelligence (AI) that allows for training machine learning models on distributed data sets.

Machine learning (ML) is the study of algorithms and statistical models that computer systems use to perform a specific task without being explicitly programmed. On the other hand, Distributed Machine Learning (DML) refers to the distribution of an ML algorithm across multiple computers or devices to work together in solving a computational problem, often involving large amounts of data. In DML, the workload is divided among multiple nodes, enabling the processing of larger data sets, faster training times, and better scalability. The main difference is that ML focuses on the algorithms, while DML focuses on their distribution and execution on multiple computers.

Deep Learning is a subset of Machine Learning that focuses on creating artificial neural networks to model and solve complex problems. These neural networks are designed to learn end-to-end, meaning they learn the mapping between input and output without requiring manual feature extraction or engineering. This allows Deep Learning algorithms to automatically identify patterns in large amounts of data and make predictions or decisions based on that data. In other words, Deep Learning is a type of Machine Learning, and Distributed Machine Learning is a way of executing Machine Learning algorithms, but the two are not synonymous.

In contrast, traditional Machine Learning algorithms often require the problem to be broken down into smaller parts. They require manual feature engineering, where the input data is transformed into a set of numerical features that can be used as input to the algorithm. These features are then combined at the final stage to solve the problem. This approach can still be effective in solving certain problems, but it can also be time-consuming and may not always lead to the best results.

Deep Learning has outperformed traditional Machine Learning in many applications, such as computer vision, natural language processing, and speech recognition, among others.

Deep Learning can improve the performance of Distributed Machine Learning in several ways. Deep Learning algorithms are designed to handle large amounts of data, making them well suited for Distributed Machine Learning. With the ability to divide the workload among multiple nodes, Distributed Machine Learning can process even larger data sets and train Deep Learning models more efficiently. Deep Learning algorithms can process high-dimensional inputs, such as images and text, making them a good fit for Distributed Machine Learning when processing these types of inputs. Deep Learning algorithms are designed to scale well in terms of the size of the input data and the number of parameters in the model. This makes them well suited for Distributed Machine Learning, where the goal is to scale the computational power and memory available to the algorithm. Deep Learning algorithms have been shown to perform well on various tasks, including image classification, natural language processing, and speech recognition. Distributed Machine Learning can leverage the strengths of Deep Learning algorithms to achieve even better performance by distributing the workload among multiple nodes.

Energy trading companies can benefit from DML in a variety of ways. First, compared to standard machine learning techniques, it enables model training on a significantly more extensive data set. This is important because the energy market is extremely complex and data-rich, and a machine learning model that is trained on a larger data set is more likely to be accurate.

Second, Deep Learning techniques (DML) tend to solve the problem end to end, whereas machine learning techniques need the problem statements broken down into different parts to be solved first, and then their results to be combined at the final stage.

Third, compared to conventional machine learning techniques, DML is more effective. This is because DML can parallelize the training process, meaning multiple models can be trained simultaneously. This is significant because it makes it possible for energy trading companies to train models more quickly, which is essential in a constantly shifting market. Fourth, DML is more flexible than traditional machine learning methods. This is because DML can be used to train various models, including deep learning models. Deep learning is a type of machine learning that is particularly well-suited to the energy market because it can handle the large and complex data sets that are characteristic of the market.

Fifth, DML is more accurate than traditional machine learning methods. This is because DML can learn from data distributed across multiple servers. This is significant because it enables energy trading companies to train models using information from many sources, which is crucial for obtaining a precise market picture. Finally, DML is more scalable than traditional machine learning methods. This is because DML can be deployed on various systems, including the cloud. This is important because it allows energy trading firms to deploy models on a large scale, which is necessary for dealing with the large and complex data sets characteristic of the market.

In conclusion, DML is a powerful tool energy trading firms can use to improve their performance. DML has several advantages, including the ability to train models on larger data sets, the ability to parallelize the training process, the ability to train a variety of different models, the ability to learn from data that is distributed across multiple servers, and the ability to deploy models on a large scale.

Digital Field Workforce

Utility companies can enhance their operations in various ways with the aid of digital field workforce solutions that leverage AI. For example, AI can be used to manage and optimize field workflows, dispatch field workers to job sites, and track and analyze field worker performance. Additionally, AI can recognize and anticipate issues in the field, including equipment failures, and offer suggestions for how to deal with them.

Digital field workforce solutions that use AI can help improve the efficiency and effectiveness of utility operations. By managing and optimizing field workflows, AI can help ensure that field workers are dispatched to the most appropriate job sites and have the information they need to complete their tasks. AI can also assist utilities in monitoring and analyzing the performance of field workers, spotting issues on the ground, and offering solutions.

Digital field workforce solutions can help improve the safety of utility workers by providing them with the information they need to avoid hazards in the field. Additionally, AI can recognize and anticipate issues in the field, including equipment failures, and offer suggestions for how to deal with them.

AI-powered digital field labor solutions can increase utility operations' effectiveness, efficiency, and safety. By managing and optimizing field workflows, dispatching field workers to job sites, and tracking and analyzing field worker performance, AI can help utilities improve their operations and ensure that their workers are safe.

Integrated Customer Analytics

In the current business scenario, customer analytics is one of the most powerful tools companies use to understand customers and make better business decisions. It can help organizations in various ways, such as reducing customer churn, improving customer satisfaction, and increasing customer loyalty.

With the advent of artificial intelligence (AI), customer analytics has become even more powerful. Organizations can use AI to automate the customer analytics process and obtain more precise and useful insights. In addition, an extensive consumer perspective is provided by integrated customer analytics, a technique that uses AI to evaluate customer data from many sources. This process can help organizations better understand the customer and make more informed decisions. Utilities greatly impact our daily lives since they supply the water and electricity needed to run our homes and businesses. However, managing these essential services can be challenging, especially for large organizations. That's where integrated customer analytics can help.

Customer analytics may provide utilities with a thorough understanding of their consumers, usage patterns, and preferences by integrating data from numerous sources. This information can be used to improve customer service, reduce costs, and make better decisions about infrastructure investments.

For example, customer analytics can help utilities identify areas of high demand, so they can plan for future needs and avoid service disruptions. To provide targeted efficiency initiatives, it can also assist them to identify places where consumers are using more energy than they should. And it can help them understand which customers are at risk of leaving for another provider, so they can take steps to keep them happy.

In short, integrated customer analytics is a powerful tool that can help utilities provide better service, lower costs, and make more informed decisions.

Future of Compliance

The future of regulatory compliance management is shrouded in potential but fraught with uncertainty. But as industries across the globe face increasing compliance pressures, many are turning to artificial intelligence (AI) for help.

By automating the compliance process, AI can free up time and resources that might be better used in other business-related areas. Additionally, AI can help identify compliance risks before they become problems and can even provide recommendations on how to mitigate those risks. Artificial Intelligence (AI) has the potential to help organizations tackle a variety of challenges, including

1. **Improving Efficiency**: AI can automate tasks previously performed by humans, freeing up time for employees to focus on higher-level work. This can lead to increased productivity and efficiency.

2. **Enhancing Customer Experience**: AI can personalize customer interactions and provide more relevant information and recommendations, leading to an improved customer experience.

3. **Streamlining Operations**: AI can analyze data from various sources to identify inefficiencies and improvement opportunities, helping organizations streamline their processes and make data-driven decisions.

4. **Reducing Costs**: AI can automate tasks previously performed by humans, reducing labor costs. Additionally, AI can help organizations make better decisions by analyzing data, leading to cost savings.

5. **Improving Decision-Making**: AI can provide organizations with valuable insights and recommendations by analyzing large amounts of data, helping decision-makers make informed decisions.

6. **Managing Risks**: AI can help organizations identify and manage risks by analyzing data and providing early warnings of potential issues.

7. **Improving Predictive Maintenance**: AI can be used to predict when equipment or machinery is likely to fail, allowing organizations to perform maintenance before a breakdown occurs.

8. **Facilitating Compliance**: AI can help organizations ensure compliance with regulations by automating compliance checks and providing real-time insights into compliance risks.

But while the potential benefits of AI are clear, the technology is still in its early stages, and there are various challenges that need to be addressed before it can truly be called a compliance game-changer.

One of the biggest challenges is data. Access to high-quality data is necessary for AI to function effectively. But in many cases, companies' data is siloed, inaccurate, or simply doesn't exist.

Another challenge is that AI is only as good as the algorithm it's based on. And right now, there are no "off-the-shelf" solutions for compliance. Each algorithm must be specially created because every business has different requirements. This is a costly and time-consuming process. Finally, there's the question of trust. Can companies trust an AI system to handle something as sensitive as compliance?

These challenges are not insurmountable, but they must be addressed before AI becomes a compliance game-changer. But for companies willing to invest the time and resources, the potential rewards are clear.

Connected Energy Service Provider

Utilities are emerging as a connected energy service provider, offering their customers a suite of energy management and efficiency services. These services are made possible by deploying smart meters and other advanced metering infrastructure and using big data and analytics to identify and target customer needs.

Utilities are well-positioned to provide these services, as they have a unique relationship with their customers and a deep understanding of their energy usage. By offering these services, utilities can help their customers save money, reduce their carbon footprint, and become more energy efficient.

The deployment of smart meters is a key enabler of these services. Energy usage data from smart meters is real time and can be utilized to spot patterns and trends. This data can be used to target specific customers with specific services that can help them save energy and money.

Utilities also use big data and analytics to identify customer needs and target their services. For example, utilities can determine which consumers are most likely to benefit from particular services by looking at data on client energy usage. This data-driven approach allows utilities to tailor their services to the specific needs of their customers.

The emergence of utilities as connected energy service providers is a positive development for the energy sector. In addition to helping consumers save money and use less energy, it gives utilities a new source of income.

Key Takeaways

- Digital transformation is critical to the future of the sector.

- Utilities will need to focus on customer experience; in this case, a frictionless customer experience is the best.

- The future of utility retail is data-driven. Getting to know the customer better and making data-driven decisions must be embedded in every facet of the business.

- Empowering the customer should be an important priority for utilities. Giving clients decision-making and experience control is a key component of customer empowerment. It also means giving them the information they need to make informed decisions.

- Utilities will need to partner with other industries and integrate better to emerge as a connected service provider.

CHAPTER 10

Transforming Mobility Through EV

The world is rapidly changing. Technological advances are transforming the way we move around; from how we commute to work to how we travel for leisure. Electric vehicles (EVs) and artificial intelligence (AI) are two of the most exciting new technologies revolutionizing how people commute and travel.

EVs are becoming increasingly popular due to their low emissions, cost-effectiveness, and convenience. AI is also transforming the way people travel by providing personalized recommendations, traffic route optimization, and even autonomous driving. Together, these two technologies are creating a new era of mobility that is more efficient, convenient, and sustainable.

In this chapter, we will explore how EVs, and AI are changing the way people move and how they are transforming mobility. We will look at the benefits these technologies bring to individuals, businesses, and society. We will also discuss the challenges that need to be addressed to make the most of this new era of mobility. Finally, we will consider the potential of EVs and AI to shape the future of mobility.

© Debashish Roy 2024
D. Roy, *AI for Utilities*, https://doi.org/10.1007/979-8-8688-0202-7_10

Introduction

Futurists like Thomas Edison predicted that electric cars would replace most modes of transportation. However, they were nearly a century behind in technology, and advancements are still required for mass-market EVs. Understanding each Industrial Revolution's market dynamics highlights the continuing conflict between electric and gasoline-powered automobiles. Electric vehicle adoption failed during the Second Industrial Revolution (1900s steel, electric, and petroleum) because of customer dynamics, expensive electricity storage technologies, and oil and gas business. However, the electric vehicle is becoming a mainstream transportation mechanism worldwide with recent technological advancements.

The global automotive industry is facing an unprecedented period of transformation. Electric vehicles (EVs) are becoming increasingly popular, with sales and market share increasing yearly. This trend is driven by a combination of factors, including government incentives, falling battery prices, and increasing consumer awareness of the benefits of EVs. The automobile industry is poised to undergo a dramatic change over the next ten years, with EVs likely to account for a sizable share of sales. This transformation will have a profound impact on the global economy, and we must understand the implications.

Electric vehicles have the potential to help drive economic growth and improve the quality of life for millions of people around the world. They are cleaner, more effective, and less expensive to fuel than gas-powered vehicles. EVs could greatly expand access to transportation, especially in rural areas where public transportation is limited or non-existent. EVs can also be built to suit the mobility needs of people with disabilities.

Electric vehicles (EVs) are poised to revolutionize the auto industry. EVs have several advantages over conventional vehicles. They are cheaper to maintain, produce no emissions, and are more energy efficient than traditional gas-powered vehicles. According to Bloomberg New Energy Finance, EVs will account for half of all cars sold by 2040. A confluence of factors, including the falling cost of batteries, increasing regulatory pressure on conventional cars, and the emergence of autonomous mobility services, drives this trend. As a result, electric vehicles are quickly becoming the preferred choice for many drivers, mainly due to their significant savings in fuel costs.

The average fuel economy for cars in the United States varies widely, with many newer models and hybrids achieving well above 18 miles per gallon (MPG). Considering this, the estimated monthly fuel cost can differ significantly. For example, a typical gasoline-powered car that averages 18 MPG could cost about $300 monthly to fill the tank, assuming average driving habits and fuel prices. In contrast, the monthly electricity cost for running an electric vehicle (EV) averages about $100 in the United States. However, the savings can be less substantial when comparing high-efficiency vehicles, such as hybrids that average 45 MPG, to electric vehicles. Transitioning from a high-MPG hybrid to an EV might yield nominal savings. It's essential to evaluate your specific circumstances, including the type of vehicle and driving habits, to accurately assess the potential monthly savings when switching to an electric vehicle. In addition to the enormous savings, electric cars are easier to maintain and often come with more extended warranties than gas-powered vehicles. Better fuel economy also means lower emissions and a healthier environment. These benefits make electric cars an obvious choice for many people, but there are some things you can do to make the switch even easier.

Artificial intelligence plays a significant role in electric vehicle adoption, supporting event-driven operations, enhancing retail and customer experiences, and shaping the future of autonomous vehicle solutions.

Charging Infrastructure Development

The development of electric vehicle (EV) charging infrastructure is a key part of enabling the widespread adoption of EVs. While many EV owners find that charging at home is the most practical option, public charging infrastructure is also required to allow for longer trips and offer backup charging choices. There are several different types of EV charging infrastructure, from Level 1 chargers that provide a slow charge using a standard 120-volt outlet to Level 2 chargers that use 240 volts for faster charging to DC fast chargers that can charge an EV in minutes rather than hours.

Governments, utilities, and private businesses have all invested in expanding charger networks, speeding up the development of EV charging infrastructure. As a result, in the United States, there are now over 46,000 public EV chargers, up from just 3500 in 2013.

Several challenges are associated with developing EV charging infrastructure at scale, including the high up-front costs, the need for coordination among multiple stakeholders, and the lack of standardization across charger types and networks. However, these challenges are being addressed by a growing number of initiatives and programs to accelerate the deployment of EV chargers.

For EVs to reach their full potential as a transportation option, adequate charging infrastructure must be developed to support them. This objective is attainable with continuous work and investment, and it will support the development of a cleaner, more sustainable transportation system – acceleration in charging infrastructure buildup.

The global surge in electric vehicle (EV) adoption poses a significant challenge due to the potential shortfall in charging infrastructure. With only about 300,000 public charging spots available worldwide – far fewer than the millions of gasoline and diesel fuel stations – the need for efficient management of these resources is critical. To tackle this issue, the research team at Artificial Lightning has developed advanced artificial intelligence (AI) algorithms designed to predict electric vehicle charging demand at specific locations and times.

This AI-driven approach allows for "scheduled charging," which means charging can be strategically timed during off-peak hours when electricity demand is lower and, importantly, when a higher proportion of renewable energy sources are feeding the grid. By optimizing the timing of EV charging, not only can energy costs be reduced, but carbon emissions associated with non-renewable power generation during peak times can also be significantly lowered. This smarter scheduling helps balance the load on the electrical grid, reducing the need for carbon-intensive energy production that would otherwise be necessary to meet peak demands.

Furthermore, by predicting and managing the times when EVs charge, congestion at public charging stations can be minimized, reducing wait times and enhancing the overall user experience. This systematic, predictive approach ensures that charging infrastructure is used more efficiently and sustainably, aligning with broader environmental goals

The power grid faces significant stress in the United States due to the growing percentage of electric cars. With the average electric car using a high amount of power compared to gasoline-powered cars, electric cars may cause strain on the grid in areas where they make up a significant percentage of the total cars on the road. Researchers have proposed that AI may be utilized to improve grid management to lessen grid stress considering the rising share of electric vehicles and the anticipated rise in adoption rates for electric vehicles. AI-enabled systems may be able to monitor the grid and react to changes in the grid to better manage and balance the load on the grid. AI may also be used to analyze historical data to predict future trends to better plan for grid changes and adjust grid management systems to optimize the grid for changes in load.

The main purpose of AI in electric vehicles (EVs) is to optimize and streamline the charging process. Advanced AI technologies enable charging stations to automatically detect the arrival of a car and initiate charging without manual intervention. More importantly, AI enhances the efficiency of the charging process itself by dynamically adjusting the current according to the specific needs of the vehicle, which can help in efficiently managing the power supply and reducing wear on the battery.

While AI does not directly increase the charging speed, it plays a crucial role in ensuring the vehicle is only plugged in for the necessary amount of time, by automatically stopping the charge when the battery is full. This feature prevents overcharging and energy waste, thereby contributing to the overall effectiveness and sustainability of the charging process.

Additionally, AI is being leveraged to improve the infrastructure of charging stations themselves, making them smarter and more responsive to both the grid's conditions and the vehicles' requirements. This integration of AI not only helps in making the charging process more user-friendly but also enhances the operational efficiency of EV charging stations.

To ensure that the automobile is aware of how much power it needs to reach its following location, systems that can connect with the vehicle are being created. In addition, AI is also being used in the development of smart grids. These grids can monitor electricity usage and adapt to the grid's needs. By doing this, they can balance out peaks and troughs in demand, ensuring enough power.

Interoperability of Charging Stations

Charging stations are machines used to recharge electric vehicles' batteries. They are also known as EV charging stations. AI can manage the interoperability of charging stations. This means that the charging stations can work together, regardless of their brand or make. This would make it easier for people to use charging stations, regardless of the brand of their electric vehicle.

AI can also be used to manage the pricing of charging stations. This means that the charging stations can charge different prices for different times of the day, depending on the demand. This would make it easier for people to use charging stations, as they would know how much it would cost to charge their electric vehicles.

Predictive Maintenance That Uses AI to Identify Potential Issues and Schedule Repairs

Large battery packs power electric vehicles. These battery packs are expensive, and their failure can cause significant inconvenience and expense.

Artificial intelligence (AI) is a tool that may be used to predict possible problems with EV batteries and set up maintenance appointments before the batteries malfunction. This can help to avoid unexpected downtime and associated costs.

To find possible problems, predictive maintenance systems employ a range of data sources, including data from the battery pack itself. The data is analyzed using AI algorithms to identify patterns that may indicate a pending issue.

Based on the severity of the problem and the availability of parts and manpower, the predictive maintenance system then develops a repair timetable. The goal is to repair the issue before it causes a battery pack to fail.

Predictive maintenance systems are still in the early stages of development, and their effectiveness is still being evaluated. However, they have the potential to significantly improve the reliability of EV battery packs and reduce the cost of ownership.

Intelligent Charging Planning

In a world where electric vehicles are becoming increasingly popular, the need for reliable and efficient EV charging infrastructure is more important than ever. One way to ensure EVs are charged in a timely and efficient manner is using intelligent EV charging scheduling.

With intelligent EV charging scheduling, EVs can be charged at times when excess energy is available on the grid. This lessens the burden on the system during high usage times and lowers energy prices. In addition, intelligent EV charging scheduling can help to prolong battery life by avoiding overcharging.

Various approaches can be used for intelligent EV charging scheduling. One approach is to charge EVs based on their predicted range. This considers factors such as the vehicle's previous driving history and expected routes. Another approach is to charge EVs based on their owner's schedule. For example, this could involve charging EVs overnight or when they are not being used.

The benefits of intelligent EV charging scheduling are clear. However, some challenges need to be considered. One challenge is the need for accurate data about the grid and EV usage patterns. Another challenge is ensuring EV owners can access charger locations and understand and use the scheduling system.

Despite these difficulties, scheduling intelligent EV charging has the potential to revolutionize the way EVs are charged. It can potentially improve grid stability, reduce energy costs, and prolong battery life. It is an important part of creating a future-proofed EV charging infrastructure.

State of Charge Prediction of EV Batteries

The State of Charge (SOC) of a battery measures the amount of charge remaining in the battery. It is typically expressed as a percentage of the total charge that the battery can hold. For example, a battery with a SOC of 50% has 50% of its charge remaining.

A battery's SOC is significant since it dictates how long it will operate before recharging. Therefore, a battery with a low SOC will need to be recharged more often than a high SOC.

There are many methods for predicting the SOC of a battery, but one of the most promising is using artificial intelligence (AI). AI-based SOC prediction algorithms can learn from past data to accurately predict the SOC of a battery in the future.

One advantage of using AI for SOC prediction is that it can consider a variety of factors that might affect the SOC of a battery. For example, AI can consider a battery's temperature, voltage, current, and capacity when predicting. Another advantage of using AI for SOC prediction is that the predictions can be made in real time. This is important because the SOC of a battery can change quickly and unexpectedly. AI can assist in preventing battery failure and extending battery life by forecasting the SOC in real time. There are many potential applications for AI-based SOC prediction. For example, AI could be used to predict the SOC of a battery in an electric vehicle (EV) so that the driver knows when to recharge the battery. AI could also be used to predict the SOC of a battery in a power grid so that operators can take steps to avoid blackouts.

AI-based SOC prediction is a promising technology with many potential applications. It can improve the efficiency of battery usage and prolong the life of batteries.

Electric Vehicle Routing Management

Electric vehicle routing management is a process of planning and optimizing the routes of electric vehicles to ensure efficient and cost-effective operations. It is a complex process that involves various factors such as the type of electric vehicle, the battery capacity, the charging infrastructure, the weather conditions, and the traffic conditions.

Electric vehicle routing management systems use artificial intelligence (AI) techniques to design efficient routes for electric vehicles. These AI algorithms consider all the relevant factors and create safe, efficient, cost-effective routes.

The use of AI in electric vehicle routing management has several advantages:

1. AI-based systems can consider many factors and create optimized routes that are not possible for humans to create.

2. AI-based systems can constantly monitor the conditions on the ground and adjust the routes accordingly. This is impossible for human planners who rely on static data.

3. AI-based systems can create customized routes for each electric vehicle, considering its specific characteristics.

The use of AI in electric vehicle routing management is still in its early stages. However, it has the potential to revolutionize the way electric vehicles are operated and managed.

Data-Driven Smart Charging

Data-driven smart charging is a type of charging method for electric vehicles (EVs) that optimizes the use of the grid by using data to determine when and how to charge each vehicle. The goal of data-driven smart charging is to minimize the overall cost of charging the EV fleet while also maximizing the use of renewable energy sources and reducing the impact on the grid.

There are many benefits to data-driven smart charging, including the following:

1. **Reduced overall charging costs**: By using data to optimize the charging of each EV, the overall cost of charging the fleet can be reduced. This is because the data can be used to determine the most efficient time to charge each vehicle, and the most cost-effective type of electricity to use.

2. **Increased use of renewable energy:** Data-driven smart charging can help to increase the overall use of renewable energy sources, such as solar and wind power. This is because the data can be used to determine when the EV fleet is most likely to be charged and, thus, when renewable energy sources are most likely to be available.

3. **Reduced impact on the grid:** Data-driven smart charging can help to reduce the impact of the EV fleet on the grid. This is because the data can be used to determine when the EV fleet is most likely to be charged and, thus, when the demand on the grid is likely to be lower.

4. **Increased flexibility:** Data-driven smart charging can increase flexibility for EV fleets. This is because the data can be used to determine the most efficient time to charge each vehicle and the most cost-effective type of electricity to use. This can help to make EV fleets more responsive to changes in demand and more adaptable to the grid's needs.

5. **Increased transparency:** Data-driven smart charging can help to increase the transparency of the EV charging process. This is because the data can be used to determine the most efficient time to charge each vehicle and the most cost-effective type of electricity to use. This can help make EV charging more transparent and easier to understand for EV fleet operators and the general public.

Data-driven smart charging is an important part of the future of electric vehicles. Data-driven smart charging can help lower the overall cost of charging the EV fleet while simultaneously maximizing the usage of renewable energy sources and minimizing the grid's effect by optimizing each EV's charging.

EV Analytics and Security

As the world progresses, data analytics is becoming increasingly relied on to make decisions. This is especially true for businesses; they need to understand their customers and what they are looking for to stay ahead of the competition. However, data analytics is not just limited to businesses – it can also be used for other purposes, such as environmentalism. In fact, EV analytics is growing in popularity as people become more aware of the need to be environmentally friendly.

EV analytics is gathering and analyzing data about electric vehicles (EVs) to better understand their impact on the environment. Many sources, including EV owners, manufacturers, and governmental organizations, can provide this information. It can be used to respond to inquiries about EVs, like how many are on the road, how frequently they are used, who owns them, and so forth. Additionally, EV analytics can be used to study the environmental impact of EVs and how they compare to other vehicles.

There are many benefits to using EV analytics. For one, it can help make EVs more popular by showing people that they are being used and that they are having a positive impact on the environment. Additionally, it can help policymakers make better decisions about incentives and regulations surrounding EVs. Finally, EV analytics can assist companies in better understanding the needs of their clients and informing marketing and product development decisions. In general, EV analytics is an effective technique that can be utilized to enhance our comprehension of electric vehicles and their environmental impact. As EVs become more popular, it will become increasingly important to use data analytics to ensure that they are being used effectively and that their environmental impact is minimized.

The deployment of electric vehicles (EVs) varies between developed and developing nations due to several factors, including infrastructure, economic development, and consumer demand.

Developed Nations:

- In developed nations, EV deployment is driven by government policies, consumer demand, and industry investments. These countries have the infrastructure, technology, and financial resources to support the widespread adoption of EVs, such as charging networks, battery production facilities, and high-tech manufacturing capabilities.

- Governments in developed nations have implemented a variety of incentives to encourage the adoption of EVs, such as tax credits, subsidies, and charging infrastructure development. These policies have helped create a favorable environment for the growth of the EV market, and consumers have responded positively, leading to increased demand for EVs.

Developing Nations:

- In contrast, the deployment of EVs in developing nations is still in the early stages and faces several challenges, including a lack of infrastructure, low consumer awareness, and limited access to financing.

- The development of charging infrastructure is a major challenge in developing nations, as the cost of building and maintaining a charging network can be prohibitively high. Moreover, this lack of infrastructure makes it difficult for consumers to adopt EVs, as they are often concerned about the availability of charging stations.

- Another factor limiting the deployment of EVs in developing nations is the limited access to financing for consumers and manufacturers. Many consumers in developing nations may not have the financial resources to purchase an EV, and manufacturers may struggle to secure funding for production and marketing.

In conclusion, deploying EVs in developed nations is driven by favorable government policies, consumer demand, and industry investments. The lack of infrastructure, low consumer awareness, and limited financing access limit EVs' deployment in developing nations.

Facial Recognition for Driver Authentication and Security

In a world where driver authentication and security are increasingly important, facial recognition using AI is becoming a more popular solution. AI can check the driver's identity and that they are permitted to drive the car by taking a picture of their face with a camera. This verification can be used to unlock the vehicle's doors, start the engine, and even authenticate the driver's identity for payment purposes.

Facial recognition is not only more convenient than traditional methods such as keys or keycards, but it is also more secure. For example, driver authentication using facial recognition is virtually impossible to spoof, making it a much more reliable verification method. Additionally, facial recognition can be used in conjunction with additional security measures like GPS tracking and geofencing to further secure vehicles and their contents.

While facial recognition is a promising solution for driver authentication and security, it is important to note that the technology is still in its early stages of development. As such, there are a few challenges that need to be addressed before it can be widely adopted. Firstly, the accuracy of facial recognition systems can vary greatly, depending on factors such as lighting and angle of view. Secondly, facial recognition systems can be fooled by masks or other objects that obscure the face. Finally, facial recognition systems can be biased against certain demographics, such as people of color or women.

Despite these challenges, facial recognition is a promising driver authentication and security solution. It is anticipated that these issues will be resolved as technology advances and facial recognition will gain popularity as a solution.

EV Charging Behavior

As the world progresses, more and more people are beginning to use electric vehicles to save on gas and help the environment. However, one of the issues that still need to be addressed is the lack of public EV charging stations. To help with this, many companies are now using AI to create better EV charging behavior.

Some ways that AI is being used to improve EV charging behavior include

1. **Optimizing routes:** AI can be used to help plan the most efficient route for EV owners, considering the location of public charging stations.

2. **Scheduling charging times:** AI can also be used to schedule charging times based on the owner's needs and power availability.

3. **Managing power usage:** AI can help to manage EV charging stations' power usage, ensuring that they are not overused and that everyone has a fair chance to charge their vehicle.

4. **Improving customer service:** AI can be used to improve customer service at EV charging stations, providing helpful information and guidance to owners.

5. **Preventing fraud:** AI can help to prevent fraud at EV charging stations by identifying suspicious behavior and alerting authorities.

Overall, AI is beginning to play a big role in improving EV charging behavior. AI simplifies charging EVs by planning routes, scheduling charging periods, and controlling power use. AI is also improving customer service and preventing fraud at EV charging stations.

Monetizing EV Operational Data

One of the most significant trends in the automotive industry right now is the electrification of automobiles. With the rise of electric vehicles (EVs), there is a growing need for new ways to monetize EV operational data using AI.

One way to monetize EV operational data is to use it to improve the efficiency of EV charging infrastructure. For example, charging infrastructure providers may better understand how EVs are being utilized and adjust their charging networks by utilizing AI to examine EV operational data. Another way to monetize EV operational data is to use it to improve the accuracy of demand-side management (DSM) programs. Utilities use DSM programs to manage the demand for electricity on the grid. Using AI to analyze EV operational data, utilities can more accurately predict when and how much electricity EVs will need and adjust their DSM programs accordingly.

Finally, EV operational data can also be used to improve the accuracy of vehicle-to-grid (V2G) services. V2G services allow EVs to provide power to the grid when there is excess demand. By using AI to analyze EV operational data, V2G service providers can better understand how EVs are used and optimize their services accordingly.

All these examples show how AI can be used to monetize EV operational data. Using AI to analyze this data, businesses can better understand how EVs are being used and optimize their services accordingly.

However, several challenges lie ahead when monetizing electric vehicle (EV) operational data. One of the main challenges in monetizing EV operational data is ensuring the privacy and security of the data. Consumers may be concerned about the potential misuse of their personal and sensitive information, and organizations must implement robust security measures to protect the data from unauthorized access and breaches. Another challenge is determining who owns and controls the data generated by EVs. In some cases, the vehicle manufacturer may own the data, while in others, the consumer may own the data. This lack of clarity can make it difficult for organizations to monetize the data.

Monetizing EV operational data requires integrating data from multiple sources, such as vehicles, charging stations, and other connected devices. However, the lack of standardization in the industry makes it difficult to ensure the interoperability of data from different sources. In addition, the monetization of EV operational data is subject to various regulations, such as data protection laws and privacy regulations. Organizations must ensure that they comply with these regulations, which can be complex and time-consuming. The monetization of EV operational data is a growing industry, and many competitors are offering similar services. Organizations must differentiate themselves in the market to succeed and compete effectively.

Creating value for consumers and monetizing vehicle data requires a multifaceted approach that involves several steps:

1. **Building Trust:** To create value for consumers, organizations must build trust by demonstrating their commitment to data privacy and security. This can be done by implementing robust data protection measures, such as encryption and secure data storage, and by being transparent about the data being collected and how it will be used.

2. **Offering Value-Added Services:** One way to create value for consumers and monetize vehicle data is by offering value-added services that leverage the data generated by EVs. For example, organizations can offer predictive maintenance services, personalized energy management services, or real-time traffic and routing services.

3. **Partnerships and Collaboration:** Organizations can also create value by partnering with other organizations in the industry, such as charging network providers or connected vehicle service providers, to create new and innovative services.

4. **Data Monetization:** Organizations can monetize vehicle data by selling it to third-party organizations, such as data analytics companies, or by using it to inform their own decision-making processes and improve their products and services.

5. **Continuously Improving Services:** To continue to create value for consumers and monetize vehicle data, organizations must continuously evolve and improve their services. This can be done by incorporating new and emerging technologies, such as artificial intelligence and machine learning, and by incorporating consumer and stakeholder feedback into the development process.

Advanced Analytics on Electric Vehicle Charging Station Usage

The electric vehicle charging station usage data set consists of data collected from electric vehicle charging stations in the United States. The data includes specifics about the number of charging sessions, their length, the kind of charger utilized, when it was utilized, and where the charger was located. The data also includes information on the vehicle make and model and the user's zip code.

As the number of electric vehicles (EVs) on the road continues to grow, so does the demand for EV charging stations. However, designing and managing a charging station network is a complex task, made even more difficult because EV charging patterns can vary significantly from one driver to the next.

To address this challenge, many EV charging station operators are turning to artificial intelligence (AI) for help. AI can be used to optimize the charging stations' operation in real time and predict when and where EV drivers will likely need to charge their vehicles. One of the most promising applications of AI for EV charging station operators is the use of data from EV charging station usage. AI systems can gain a lot of knowledge about EV driver behavior by evaluating this data, and they can use this information to increase the effectiveness of charging station operations. For example, AI-powered systems can identify charging patterns indicative of driver anxiety about range and adjust charging station operations accordingly.

AI can also be used to monitor EV charging station usage data to identify potential problems, such as overloaded circuits or stations that are not being used as much as expected. As a result, AI can assist in making sure that EV drivers always have access to the necessary charging infrastructure by promptly addressing these problems. AI is anticipated to become even more crucial to managing EV charging station networks in the future. As the number of EVs on the road continues to grow, so will the demand for charging infrastructure, and AI will be essential for managing this demand efficiently and effectively.

Key Takeaways

- EV adoption is not just about vehicle technology, it's about an entire ecosystem of cities, utilities, and companies that must work together.

- There is a business case for EVs, and it will only get stronger as the cost of batteries comes down.

- The transportation sector is responsible for significant greenhouse gas emissions, and EVs can help reduce those emissions.

- Infrastructure is a critical piece of the EV puzzle, and cities and utilities are working to build it up.

- Consumer education is also key to EV adoption, and many resources are available to help people understand the benefits of EVs.

CHAPTER 11

Age of DERs

The dawn of the Age of Distributed Energy Resources (DERs) is upon us. Once dismissed as too expensive and unstable, DERs are now considered reliable, sustainable, and cost-effective energy sources. From large-scale solar farms to microgrids powering individual households, DERs are revolutionizing how we think about energy production, consumption, and storage. In this chapter, we will discuss the future of DER systems and how AI will play a role.

Introduction

The need for more efficient and environmentally friendly energy sources in a rapidly developing world has never been greater. One promising solution is the use of distributed energy resources (DER), which are small-scale technologies that generate electricity at or near where it will be used. Costs for Distributed Energy Resources (DER) continue to fall, and standards continue to progress, and, of course, new DER interconnections continue to take place. The future of DER has never looked better. Still the uncertainty that it brings to the utility industry is a challenge that needs to be continually addressed collaboratively.

The future may likely include much more integration of DER into utility systems and interaction between the consumer and the utility. How the utility industry can better prepare now for this future is an important topic for discussion. Ratepayer advocates and other organizations are pressing for affordability and fairness issues to take center stage as

© Debashish Roy 2024
D. Roy, *AI for Utilities*, https://doi.org/10.1007/979-8-8688-0202-7_11

California regulators launch a comprehensive effort to prepare the electric grid for an anticipated flood of electric vehicles and other distributed energy resources (DERs). California is bracing for considerable increases in DERs on the grid over the next decade behind-the-meter solar, behind-the-meter storage, and electric vehicle demand are expected to increase by 260%, 770%, and 370%, respectively, from 2019 to 2030, according to regulatory forecasts.

Distributed energy resources (DERs) are energy resources that are geographically dispersed, like rooftop solar panels, or that are non-traditional and non-centralized, like electric vehicles (EVs).

DERs are one of the promising options for environmentally friendly energy sources because they can help to reduce greenhouse gas emissions and mitigate the impacts of climate change. By producing energy at or near the point of consumption, DERs can reduce the need for long-distance transmission and distribution of energy, which is often associated with high energy losses and greenhouse gas emissions.

In addition, DERs can improve energy security and resilience by reducing dependence on large-scale energy generation facilities, which can be vulnerable to disruptions or failures. By providing a distributed and decentralized energy source, DERs can help ensure a more stable and secure energy supply. Furthermore, DERs can help to create local economic benefits by generating revenue for the owners of the systems and by creating jobs in the renewable energy sector. By providing a source of clean energy, DERs can also help reduce energy costs for consumers and contribute to energy independence and self-sufficiency.

DERs can play an important role in the operation of EVs by reducing their carbon footprint, improving energy management, and enhancing the integration of renewable energy into the energy system. By utilizing DERs, EVs can become a more environmentally friendly and sustainable mode of transportation. DERs can be used to charge EVs by integrating renewable energy sources, such as solar or wind power, into charging stations. This can help reduce EVs' carbon footprint by reducing the dependence on grid-based electricity, which is often generated from fossil fuels. DERs can also be utilized through V2G technology, which allows EVs to supply excess energy back to the grid. This can help balance the grid's energy demand and supply and reduce the need for additional power plants.

DERs can be integrated into the energy management system of EVs to optimize energy use and reduce energy costs. For example, by using the information on the battery state of charge, driving patterns, and renewable energy generation, the energy management system can optimize the use of renewable energy and minimize the need to purchase grid-based electricity. In addition, the batteries in EVs can also be used as DERs by using them for energy storage. This can help to store excess energy generated from renewable sources, such as solar or wind power, and use it to power EVs or supply it back to the grid.

Energy storage, combined heat and power, microgrids, and distributed generation are commonly used to describe distributed energy resources. These resources are installed at the customer site, often at or near the load, and operate independently of the main electrical grid. Due to their location, they can respond more quickly to changes in demand and are often co-located with renewable energy sources, such as solar panels.

AI in DER

Through proactive equipment maintenance, real-time grid monitoring, and automated control of DER resources, AI can significantly improve the utilization of DER. Predictive maintenance of DER equipment can help to avoid costly downtime and ensure that resources are used as efficiently as possible. Artificial intelligence (AI) can be used to keep an eye out for wear and tear on equipment and forecast when repair or replacement is likely to be required. The utilization of DER resources can be maximized, and blackouts can be avoided with the use of real-time grid condition monitoring. AI can be used to monitor power usage and demand and predict when demand is likely to exceed supply. This information can be used to automatically control DER resources, such as turning on backup generators or curtailing power usage.

Automated control of DER resources can help to optimize power generation and usage and reduce the need for manual intervention. AI can be used to automatically adjust the output of DER resources in response to changes in demand, weather conditions, and other factors. This can help to ensure that power is generated and used efficiently and that resources are used as effectively as possible.

DER Planning

Uncertainty Modeling of Distributed Energy Resources

Integrating Distributed Energy Resources (DERs) into the grid is challenging because of the inherent variability and uncertainty of these resources. Therefore, accurate DER models that can anticipate its output under different circumstances are crucial for efficient grid management. Artificial intelligence (AI) techniques can be used to create accurate models of DERs. One approach is to use a neural network (NN) to learn the relationship between the input (e.g., weather conditions) and output (e.g., power output) of the DER. Another approach is to use a support vector machine (SVM) to create a model that can predict the output of the DER under different conditions.

Both AI techniques are effective in modeling DERs. However, there is still some ambiguity regarding how well these models will function in actual use. This uncertainty can be reduced by using a combination of multiple AI techniques. For example, it is possible to develop a more accurate model of the DER that can better handle the unpredictability and uncertainty of the resource by combining a NN and SVM. Geographic decision support systems powered with AI can optimize the placement of distributed energy resources.

Geographic decision support systems (GDSS) are designed to help organizations optimize the placement of distributed energy resources (DER) using artificial intelligence (AI). By considering factors such as load, topography, weather, and infrastructure, GDSS can help identify the most efficient placement of DERs to meet the energy needs of a specific area.

In many cases, AI-based GDSS can provide more accurate results than traditional optimization methods. This is because AI can more quickly and easily identify patterns and relationships that would be difficult for humans to discern. As a result, AI-based GDSS can help organizations save time and money by reducing the need for trial-and-error when placing DERs.

In addition to optimizing DER placement, GDSS can help forecast energy demand, assess the impact of proposed energy projects, and monitor changes in the energy landscape. Organizations may make better choices regarding their energy strategy with the support of GDSS, which offers insights into the future of energy demand.

Quantifying Rooftop Photovoltaic Solar Energy Potential: A Machine Learning Approach

There is a growing interest in incorporating artificial intelligence (AI) into the analysis of renewable energy sources, such as solar photovoltaic (PV) systems. AI can be used to predict the output of PV systems and to optimize their performance. In this way, AI can help unlock rooftop PV systems' full potential.

The use of AI in the analysis of rooftop PV potential can help to improve the accuracy of estimates. For example, AI can be used to identify the best orientation and tilt for PV panels, considering the local climate. AI can also be used to predict the amount of shading a PV system will experience and to optimize the layout of PV panels to minimize shading.

In addition to improving the accuracy of estimates, AI can also help optimize PV systems' performance. For example, AI can automatically adjust the PV inverters' settings to maximize energy output. AI can also be used to monitor the performance of PV systems in real-time and to identify and diagnose problems.

The use of AI in the analysis of rooftop PV potential can help to make the most of this renewable energy resource. In doing so, AI can play a key role in transitioning to a low-carbon future.

Machine Learning for Solar Irradiance Forecasting of Photovoltaic System

Solar irradiance forecasting uses machine learning algorithms to predict the amount of solar radiation a photovoltaic (PV) system will receive. A range of potential values for sun irradiation can be provided in a probabilistic forecast, which can be generated for a specific location and time. Solar irradiance forecasting is a valuable tool for PV system operators, as it can help them schedule maintenance and repairs and optimize the system's output. In addition to assisting with integrating the PV system into the grid, the forecast can be used to estimate the quantity of power the system will produce.

Solar irradiance forecasting is a relatively new field, and there is still much research to be done to improve the forecasts' accuracy. However, using machine learning algorithms to make projections is a promising strategy, and it's possible that as more data is gathered and more expertise is gained, the forecasts will become more accurate.

DER Generation

Autonomous Energy Grids: Controlling the Future Grid with Large Amounts of Distributed Energy Resources

The electric grid is a power generation, transmission, and distribution facility network that delivers electricity to customers. The grid is a complex system that must be operated and maintained to ensure reliability and safety.

The traditional electric grid is transforming due to the increasing penetration of renewable energy sources, such as wind and solar, and the rise of distributed energy resources (DERs), such as storage and demand response. This transformation is enabled by advances in digital technology, which provide new capabilities for monitoring, managing, and controlling the grid.

One of the critical challenges in this transformation is maintaining grid reliability and security while accommodating the variability of renewable energy sources and the distributed nature of DERs. This challenge is being addressed by developing autonomous energy grids that use artificial intelligence (AI) to control the flow of electricity on the grid.

AI-enabled energy grids can learn from data and adapt to changing conditions in real-time. This enables them to provide reliable and secure power delivery even as the mix of energy sources and the distribution of resources on the grid change.

Although the use of AI in energy grids is still in its infancy, several pilot projects are already underway that showcase this technology's potential. For example, in Germany, a consortium of utilities and technology companies uses AI to control the flow of electricity on a virtual power plant that includes more than 1000 DERs. The project demonstrates that AI can manage a complex power system in real time and provide grid services, such as balancing, that centralized power plants traditionally offer.

In the United States, the Department of Energy's Argonne National Laboratory is developing an AI-enabled microgrid that can operate autonomously to provide power during grid outages. In addition, critical loads like hospitals and emergency shelters will be powered by the microgrid using a combination of solar, thermal, and storage resources. These pilot projects are just the beginning of the potential for AI in energy grids. As the technology matures, it is anticipated that as technology develops, it will become more crucial to the operation of the electric grid.

Data-Driven Secondary Control of Distributed Energy Resources

The 21st century has seen an increase in the use of data-driven methods to control various systems. One such system is the distribution of energy resources. The use of data-driven methods can help to optimize the distribution of these resources and make the system more efficient.

In the past, the distribution of energy resources was controlled by primary controllers. These controllers oversaw making sure that the resources were allocated securely and effectively. However, they could not consider the system's changing needs. This often led to inefficient distribution of resources.

Data-driven methods can help to address this problem. By using data to control the distribution of resources, the system can be more responsive to the system's changing needs. This can lead to a more efficient distribution of resources and can help to reduce the overall cost of the system.

Data-driven methods can also help to improve the safety of the system. The principal controllers can be made aware of possible issues before they arise by using data to monitor the system. This can help to prevent accidents and can make the system more reliable.

The use of data-driven methods is not without its challenges. One challenge is that data can be difficult to collect and process. In addition, data can be misinterpreted, which is another problem. This may result in the distribution of resources being decided upon incorrectly. Despite these difficulties, data-driven approaches have certain benefits that make them ideal for managing the distribution of energy resources. These methods can help to optimize the system and make it more efficient. They can also help to improve the safety of the system.

Load Modeling and Non-intrusive Load Monitoring to Integrate Distributed Energy Resources in Low- and Medium-Voltage Networks

The electric grid is a power generation, transmission, and distribution facility network that delivers electricity to customers. The grid is a complex system that must be operated and maintained to ensure reliability and safety.

The traditional electric grid is transforming due to the increasing penetration of renewable energy sources, such as wind and solar, and the rise of distributed energy resources (DERs), such as storage and demand response. This transformation is enabled by advances in digital technology, which provide new capabilities for monitoring, managing, and controlling the grid.

One of the critical challenges in this transformation is maintaining grid reliability and security while accommodating the variability of renewable energy sources and the distributed nature of DERs. This challenge is being addressed by developing autonomous energy grids that use artificial intelligence (AI) to control the flow of electricity on the grid.

AI-enabled energy grids can learn from data and quickly adapt to changing conditions. This enables them to provide reliable and secure power delivery even as the mix of energy sources and the distribution of resources on the grid change.

DER Operation and Security

A Battery-Based Authentication Scheme for Distributed Energy Resources

We assume that each DER is equipped with a battery, and the battery can be used to store the energy generated by the DER. The proposed scheme is based on the fact that the energy stored in the battery can be used to power the DER, and the DER can be authenticated using the energy stored in the battery.

The proposed scheme has the following advantages:

1) The scheme is scalable since the number of batteries does not limit the number of DERs authenticated.

2) The scheme is robust since the energy stored in the battery can be used to power the DER even if the DER is not connected to the grid.

3) The scheme is secure since the energy stored in the battery cannot be used to authenticate other DERs.

4) The scheme is efficient since the energy stored in the battery can be used to power the DER for a long period.

5) The scheme is flexible since the DER can be authenticated using different authentication algorithms.

Interconnection Protection of Distributed Energy Resources Using Intelligent Schemes

A crucial problem in the electricity system is the interconnection protection of distributed energy resources (DER). Renewable energy resources, energy storage systems, and microgrids may all be a part of the DER. The traditional protection schemes cannot provide optimized and intelligent protection for the DER. The AI-based intelligent schemes can provide optimized and intelligent protection for the DER. The DER and power system features can be learned by the AI-based schemes, and they can then use this knowledge to decide whether to defend a system or not. The AI-based schemes can learn the DER and power system features, and they can then use this knowledge to decide whether to defend a system or not. AI-based techniques can enhance the protective capabilities of the DER. The AI-based schemes can also provide self-adaptive protection for the DER. The AI-based schemes can learn the changes in the DER and the power system make the protection decision accordingly.

AI-based schemes can provide optimized protection for the DER. The number of false alerts and misoperation of the protective devices can be reduced using AI-based methods. The AI-based schemes can also provide coordinated protection for the DER. The AI-based schemes can coordinate the protection devices of the DER to provide optimized protection.

The AI-based schemes can provide self-learning protection for the DER. The AI-based schemes can determine a protective strategy based on their knowledge of the DER and power system features. The AI-based schemes can also provide self-adaptive protection for the DER. The AI-based schemes can learn the changes in the DER and the power system and make the protection decision accordingly.

Key Takeaways

- Distributed energy resource penetrates the overall energy ecosystem at a rapid pace.

- AI will play an important role in seamlessly integrating the DER into the core energy ecosystem and smoothening the uncertainty.

- Integrating distributed energy resources (DERs) and artificial intelligence (AI) can help create a more efficient, sustainable, and resilient electricity grid.

- AI has the potential to transform the electricity grid and the way we manage our distributed energy resources in the future.

- AI can be used to improve the power system's resilience and to reduce the risk of blackouts and other disruptions.

CHAPTER 12

Utilities in the Metaverse

The use of Metaverse in the utility sector is a rapidly growing trend that has seen a marked increase in recent years. This technology has the potential to revolutionize the utility sector, as it can provide faster, more reliable, and more secure services. This chapter will discuss the advantages and potential applications of Metaverse in the utility sector and how it can be used to improve customer experience, reduce costs, and increase efficiency.

Introduction

The Metaverse is coined by science fiction writer Neal Stephenson in his 1992 novel Snow Crash. It is a blockchain-based virtual reality (VR) environment with avatars as its inhabitants. The Metaverse is a user-created virtual world that exists on the Internet. It is a 3D space where users can interact with each other and create their content. The Metaverse is similar to other virtual worlds, such as Second Life, but it is unique in that it is entirely user-created. This means that anyone can create their world within the Metaverse, and there are no limits to what can be created. The Metaverse is constantly evolving and expanding as new users add their creations.

The Metaverse is a place where people can be anyone they want to be. There are no rules or restrictions on what users can do or create. Because of this, it's a fantastic location for people to discover their creativity and interact with new people from around the globe. In addition, the Metaverse is a fantastic environment for information sharing and learning new skills. There are many user-created tutorials and resources available, and users can also learn from each other through trial and error. The Metaverse is constantly changing and expanding, and it is impossible to predict what it will look like in the future. However, one thing is certain: the Metaverse is an amazing place that allows users to interact with each other in previously impossible ways.

Metaverse refers to a virtual shared space, typically with a high degree of user interactivity, and sometimes including the ability for users to represent themselves through virtual avatars. The concept of a Metaverse has been popularized in various forms of science fiction. It is now being explored as a potential future development of the Internet and the convergence of real and virtual reality. It is envisioned as a decentralized and immersive virtual world where users can engage in various activities, from socializing to commerce and gaming.

In the movie starring Keanu Reeves, "The Matrix," the Metaverse refers to a simulated reality created by sentient machines in which most of humanity is unknowingly trapped. The Matrix serves as a means of control and energy source for the machines, while the human mind is connected to the simulation and experiences it as reality. The term "Metaverse" in this context refers to a virtual world that is parallel to the physical world. The concept of a Metaverse in "The Matrix" has been widely discussed and has significantly impacted popular culture, influencing the way people think about virtual reality and the nature of reality itself.

Training in the Metaverse

Virtual Reality (VR) technology has the potential to significantly improve the training model for utilities by providing a highly immersive and interactive learning experience. Here are some ways in which VR can improve the training model:

1. **Hands-on Training**: VR simulations can provide a realistic and safe environment for workers to practice and test their skills, reducing the risk of accidents and mistakes in real-life scenarios.

2. **Enhanced Realism**: VR simulations can recreate real-life situations, equipment, and processes in a highly detailed and accurate manner, allowing workers to experience and practice their responses to various scenarios.

3. **Scalability**: VR technology allows for training to be delivered to many workers simultaneously, regardless of location, reducing the costs and time required for traditional in-person training.

4. **Improved Retention**: VR simulations can create an engaging and memorable learning experience, helping workers retain and recall information more effectively.

5. **Customizable Training**: VR simulations can be easily modified to match specific training needs, making it possible to train workers on specific tasks and scenarios relevant to their jobs.

Overall, VR technology has the potential to revolutionize the training model for utilities, making it more efficient, effective, and engaging for workers.

However, the question that looms in the minds of individuals is, how do you safely train personnel working on and around dangerous, high-voltage substation equipment without exposing them to actual danger during training? The answer is Virtual Reality.

Virtual Reality (VR) technology can safely train personnel working on and around dangerous, high-voltage substation equipment without exposing them to actual danger during training. Here are some ways VR can be used for this purpose:

1. **Simulation-Based Training**: VR simulations can recreate real-life situations, equipment, and processes in a highly detailed and accurate manner, allowing workers to practice and test their skills in a safe virtual environment.

2. **Hands-on Practice**: VR simulations provide a realistic and safe environment for workers to practice procedures and responses to emergencies, reducing the risk of accidents and mistakes in real-life scenarios.

3. **Interactive and Engaging**: VR simulations can create an immersive and engaging learning experience, helping workers retain and recall information more effectively.

4. **Reduced Costs and Time**: VR technology allows for training to be delivered to many workers simultaneously, regardless of location, reducing the costs and time required for traditional in-person training.

5. **Customizable Training**: VR simulations can be easily modified to match specific training needs, making it possible to train workers on specific tasks and scenarios relevant to their jobs.

Burns & McDonnell, an engineering, architecture, and construction firm headquartered in Kansas City, Missouri, has launched a new virtual reality (VR) training program for utility personnel. Utilizing virtual reality (VR) technology, the software will present accurate simulations of numerous work settings and scenarios that utility staff may face. The program aims to increase productivity and safety by giving employees a greater grasp of their surroundings and any potential hazards they may encounter. Burns & McDonnell has a long history of working with the utility industry, dating back to its founding in 1898. The company has worked on projects such as the Hoover Dam and the Kansas City Power & Light Company's coal-fired power plant. More recently, Burns & McDonnell has been involved in developing smart grid technologies and renewable energy projects. The launch of the VR training program is part of Burns & McDonnell's commitment to innovation in the utility industry. The company believes VR can provide a more immersive and effective training experience than traditional methods such as lectures or videos. Burns & McDonnell believes VR can help cut expenses by lowering the need for travel and time away from work in addition to increasing safety.

San Diego Gas and Electric Virtual Reality for Immersive Learning

SDG&E's digital innovation team used virtual reality to create a safe and realistic training environment for Journeymen Linemen. The VR experience helped employees hone their abilities in a secure environment and boosted their capacity to react to emergencies in the real world. A Virtual Reality training environment was developed to teach field workers how to identify and respond to potential utility-related wildfires. The software allows employees to simulate different situations to better understand the risks that can occur and address them more quickly.

The use of virtual reality in training can provide a more immersive and varied experience that can supplement traditional classroom and field training. This can help workers continually build skills and allow instructors to identify learning trends. In addition, technology allows workers to train in a safe environment and receive instant feedback on their performance.

Augmenting Field Workforce

The potential uses of augmented reality (AR) in field service have drawn more attention because of the technology's growth. AR has the potential to improve efficiency and accuracy in several ways, from providing real-time visualizations of data to helping workers find and identify parts. Additionally, AR can be utilized to provide a more immersive and engaging customer experience, as well as to train and support field service personnel.

Some field service organizations are already using AR to provide many benefits. For example, Telstra, a leading telecommunications company in Australia, uses AR to provide technicians with real-time visualizations of underground cables, helping them easily locate and repair faults. Similar to this, John Deere, a major producer of agricultural equipment, uses augmented reality to give technicians real-time visuals of equipment parts as well as step-by-step instructions for repairs. There are a few other potential applications of AR in field service, and we will likely see more and more organizations adopting this technology in the coming years.

Marketing of Utility Services

Utility services are necessary for the functioning of modern society, such as electricity, gas, water, waste management, etc. In recent years, there has been a trend toward using virtual worlds as a platform for marketing these kinds of services.

There are several advantages to using virtual worlds for marketing utility services. First off, unlike traditional marketing techniques, virtual worlds provide a highly immersive and dynamic environment that can be used to engage with potential clients. Secondly, virtual worlds can be used to create realistic simulations of the services offered, which can help potential customers understand their benefits. Finally, virtual worlds offer a large and growing potential customer base, which is difficult to reach through other channels.

There are many ways in which virtual worlds can be used to market utility services. Making a virtual version of the provided service, such as a water treatment facility or power plant, is one typical strategy. This can be used to provide potential customers with a realistic understanding of how the service works and how it can benefit them. Another strategy is to develop a virtual environment where potential users can test the service before utilizing it in the real world. This can be an effective way of demonstrating the value of the service and building trust with potential customers.

Whatever strategy is employed, it is critical to make sure that the virtual environment is user-friendly and well-designed, as this will significantly impact whether potential customers are eager to interact with it. In addition, the virtual world should be regularly updated with new content and features to keep users engaged and ensure sustained interest.

Key Takeaways

- The metaverse is an exciting technology, and there is significant early enthusiasm surrounding it within the utility industry.

- Metaverse can play an important role in new ways of operating the critical infrastructure operation and training utility workforce.

- Investing in the metaverse will require a robust IT infrastructure, powered by a metaverse-ready network and advanced AI technologies.

Index

A

Advanced metering infrastructure (AMI), 128–129, 133–134, 153

Agility software, 54–56

AI Adoption Maturity Model, 71
experimenting, 72
exploring phase, 72
formalizing, 72
optimizing, 72
transforming, 73

Alternative Current (AC), 2, 136

Anomaly detection, 128, 129, 132

Application-based IDS (AIDS), 134

Artificial intelligence (AI), 4, 42, 45, 49, 57, 86, 94, 104–106, 111–113, 119, 123, 125, 130, 134, 137, 140, 155, 156, 163, 180, *See also* Electric vehicles (EVs)
challenges, 151, 152
climate change, 22
DERs, 179, 180
electricity, 26
factors, 65–67
organizational factors, 68–71

traditional methods, 64
utility industry, 10, 11
wait-or-adopt syndrome, 63

Asset analytics
drone, 126
recommendations, 123, 124
RUL, 122, 123
utility poles, 124, 125

Asset management, 4, 121–122

Asset performance management (APM), 121, 122

Assets inspection, drone, 127, 128

Augmented reality (AR), 196

Augmenting human talent, 57–60

Automation, 50, 63, 92, 105, 126, 137

Autonomous energy grids, 183–185

B

Battery-based authentication, 186–188

Battery technologies, 94, 95

Behavioral models, 127, 128

Bioenergy, 91–93

Blockchain technology, 98

Boiler Turbine Generators (BTG), 105

C

D